Our Fair Share

Colin Dwyer

ISBN: 978-0-6489345-0-9

Our Fair Share is dedicated to the people of North Queensland and Regional Australia.

CONTENTS

ACKNOWLEDGMENTS

I would like to thank Tracy for her support and editing skills. Tony for his foreword. Peter for his enthusiastic encouragement.

…….and every politician, economist and journalist who has used Our Fair Share.

Foreword by Journalist Tony Raggatt

Colin Dwyer is an educated, articulate and shrewd advocate for North Queensland.

For more than 20 years this Townsville-based economist has been writing newspaper columns, compiling public submissions and providing commentary on the affairs of the day in countless print, radio and television interviews.

As he notes in this book, Our Fair Share or Our Own State, he has contributed in some way to more than 1000 stories in the region's major daily newspaper The Townsville Bulletin.

His areas of contribution have been broad.

He has covered the region's trends in population and employment growth and charted the major projects along with the jobs and investment they provide.

He has argued on the need for social infrastructure and investment into income-producing assets and provided ideas on how we can further develop our manufacturing, mining, agriculture and tourism industries.

He has kept tabs on food prices, mobilising volunteers to check on the cost of a basket of everyday household items on sale in our major supermarkets, and called on politicians to tackle the ongoing problem of escalating and unaffordable general property insurance in northern Australia.

Perhaps most of all he has advocated on the critical need for more local decision making and the establishment of a new state of North Queensland.

He has demanded fairer representation in a state where one million people live above the Tropic of Capricorn and yet more than 80 per cent of its Members of Parliament are based in the south.

Mr Dwyer has examined State Government budgets, charting the region's share of capital spending for well over a decade.

His findings that the North has been consistently short-changed in comparison with its economic contribution has not been well received in the south.

Politicians and journalists have decried his findings in articles in Brisbane's Courier Mail, pointing to the substantial annual subsidies being paid by the State's taxpayers towards delivering retail electricity prices which aren't even remotely similar to those being paid in the South East Corner.

This has only served to highlight the significant disparities which exist, the lack of investment in generation in the north and the way electricity pricing is structured with a regional node based on Brisbane favouring people living in the south.

It is telling, too, that since the first stage of Queensland's largest dam was built by the Federal Government on the Burdekin River almost 40 years ago little or nothing has been done except to collect the revenue it provides in water sales to the agricultural sector, to the city of Townsville and to the coal mines around Moranbah.

This is despite the fact that the Burdekin Falls Dam has remarkable potential for further development of its storage capacity and in the generation of hydro-electric power.

State investments occurring now into developing an urban water supply pipeline for Townsville to connect to open irrigation channels from the dam are long overdue.

Importantly, Dwyer has highlighted the need not only for social infrastructure such as those that support improvements in our lifestyle and which have been made into our health and education sectors but into income-producing assets that help to build economies.

Too often governments overlook the long-term investments needed in enabling infrastructure and in research and development which can support the economic growth of regions like North Queensland.

Dwyer's work has highlighted the increasing disconnect between the large economic contributions made by North Queensland through its mining and agricultural wealth and the declining and diminishing rates of population growth in its towns and cities.

Dwyer has made a significant contribution to understanding the problems which have long frustrated people living in regional Australia and to providing practical solutions to some of the issues which continue to shackle regional people to this day.

In that sense, this book is an important body of work.

Journalist

Tony Raggatt

1 INTRODUCTION

This book describes the origins of Our Fair Share, provides an explanation of the Our Fair Share method and its diverse application and substantial influence. It is based on published works, printed in the Townsville Bulletin from 2013 to 2015.

The book is categorised into six sections: Origins of Our Fair Share, Population and Society, Tourism, Politics, Economics, and an appendix which examines the influence of the concept and a contemporary New State Test.

Each column is a reflection of an event or issue that was topical for Townsville, north Queensland and regional Queensland, at the time.

While each column was important as a single issue, each column was also part of the whole Our Fair Share concept. Combined they form a multi-dimensional narrative, developed to educate, influence and prosecute for better outcomes for the people of Townsville, Regional Queensland and my definition of North Queensland.

Our Fair Share was originally intended as a time-saving economic tool that was part of a regional economic indicator dashboard. But it has evolved into much more.

2 Part One-The History of Our Fair Share

Our Fair Share is Regional Horizontal Fiscal Equalisation, by a simpler name.

Horizontal Fiscal Equalisation (HFE)

The Commonwealth Grants Commission defines HFE as follows: State governments should receive funding from the Commonwealth such that, if each made the same effort to raise revenue from its own sources and operated at the same level of efficiency, each would have the capacity to provide services at the same standards. Thus HFE seeks to ensure that each State has the capacity to provide services at national average levels at average levels of efficiency. HFE is grounded in the concept that citizens in different States should have access to equal standards of government services (and facilities) (sic).

Another related economic term is Vertical Fiscal Imbalance—the imbalance between the spending responsibilities of each tier of government and the own-source revenue resources available to that tier. (Source: APH)

It seemed to me, a regional economist who lives in

a regional location, that there was a gap in economic vocabulary. The definition used to allocate funding, does not include regions, their contributions, and their service and facility needs. Regional Horizontal Fiscal Equalisation (RHFE) is therefore based on the above HFE definition. However, my definition includes facilities, public investment, population and economic contribution (tax and royalties) and their changes. Regional Horizontal Fiscal Equalisation is a 'boring economic term', so, I created the term 'Our Fair Share'.

Our Fair Share became more than an economic term used by academics and public servants; it became a concept that somebody without training in economics could understand. For this reason, it has been adopted and used by regions, leaders, politicians and journalists more than economists, public administrators and academics.

Our Fair Share has become an Econ-Political term that is widely used, because it simplifies a technical term. However it has complexity.

The Our Fair Share formula involves population share, population growth and economic contribution and growth. I weight these variables in the Our Fair Share formula.

Our Fair Share is a tool that allows people and regions to compare their contribution to what they and other regions receive from state and federal governments. It's part of an arsenal of economic and political tools that prosecute a case for not just contemporary fairness, but future fairness and if the data is available, retrospective fairness. It's part of a jigsaw puzzle of information that helps decision makers make the most informed decisions and importantly, it's a political tool.

The OFS formula is reflected in the catergories of articles in this book.

OFS= economics + politics + social + other.

The economics component is defined as comparative temporal regional economic contribution, comparative temporal public investment and their change.

The political component is defined as (Framing and Wedging) * (Local Issues-outside influence + or - opposing strategy).

The social component is comparative population size and change and all the issues regional people have that are different to city people.

The other component is the unforeseen elements and the way someone manages these issues.

Data source

The primary source for Our Fair Share economic data is **Queensland Budget Paper 3, Appendix C**. This provides evidence of state government intentions to invest in Queensland by designated regions.

There are several challenges with this data source. It doesn't explicitly identify when the investment will take place. There is still no source that provides information on actual expenditure. If there is a change in costs, there is no source to identify the change. There is also a contingency allowance element that has grown substantially over the past two decades. There is no transparency about what happens to this contingency amount. It's also important to acknowledge that federal budget allocations on the whole are given to state governments for the state to manage and invest. This can create inefficiency's in economic development.

The primary source for the social component is ABS regional population estimates

Political information is gathered from anecdotal sources, media and politicians.

Our Fair Share has become part of Australian political narrative. By 2008, the term Our Fair Share starts to appear more regularly in print, TV news and Radio media platforms. I was being interviewed by journalists from all over Queensland, in particular local Newspaper, TV and radio journalists, sometimes this occurred every second day with multiple channels. I eventually contributed almost one thousand comments and articles to Townsville Bulletin (source Tony Raggatt Townsville Bulletin Journalist) and possibly similar contribution in regional and Brisbane papers. Similarly there was an enormous contribution via TV news channels and radio interviews.

In 2008 I wrote the following media information after the State budget.

Capital Punishment

State Budget night in Brisbane and Premier Anna Bligh stands in front of a group of journalists and boasts that "This year's budget delivers for the people of Townsville." There was resounding laughter and disbelief from the crowd of journalists. 1,600km away in Townsville, there was no scoffing laughter, just disappointment at the arrogance of the statement; the people who live in Townsville had been undervalued - yet again.

Local Economist Colin Dwyer said "The fact is that since the last election, the State Government has consistently shown economic disrespect for Townsville's people and their contribution to Queensland's prosperity and society. "

In 2008 the State Government produced the worst public investment performance of any budget in the last nine years, as the region lost out by 2.5% when compared to its share of economic contribution. What this means is this share of money, this investment in our current facilities, this investment in our sustainable future, is being spent elsewhere.

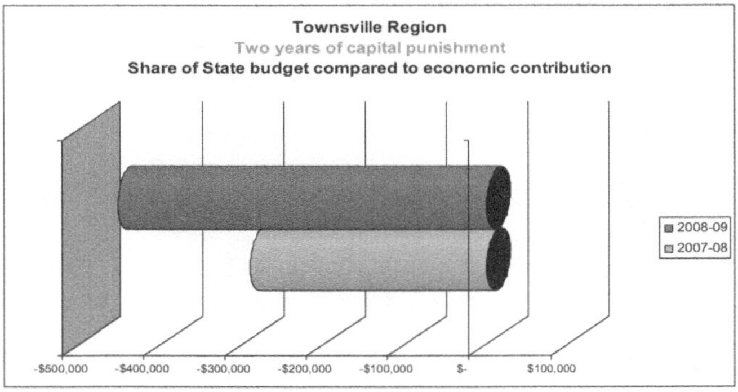

Source QLD Treasury Budget papers, AECgroup

When we analyse the previous 2 years capital allocations from state budgets, it reveals that region-wide, non-economic capacity building components of public investment have dominated the plans of the state government. Multiple correctional facility projects have dominated public investment in the past triennium.

Why Townsville should be established as the correctional facility capital of North Queensland and possibly Queensland should be questioned. Indeed, the amount spent on all these new correctional facilities over the last three years could have built a sustainable base load power station. A sustainable base load power station would have attracted additional quality sustainable industry and provided meaningful employment for future generations. We need to question the intention of the state government for our region.

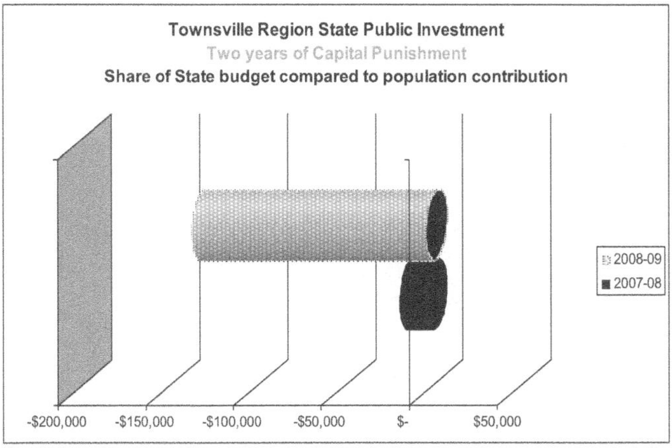

Source QLD Treasury Budget papers, ABS, DS Economics

In July 2008 I wrote a long-term analysis of State Public Investment in Northern Statistical Division (now Townsville Region).

Long term State Budget Capital Allocations 2001-2008

Capital allocations for Northern Division relative to economic contribution have been negative for six of the past (sic) nine years. Interestingly those years where allocations have been better than economic contributions were all election related years. When we analyse theses budgets, we find that regional servicing components allocated to Townsville, tend to dominate public investment and allocations are usually concentrated in less than 20% of the portfolios.

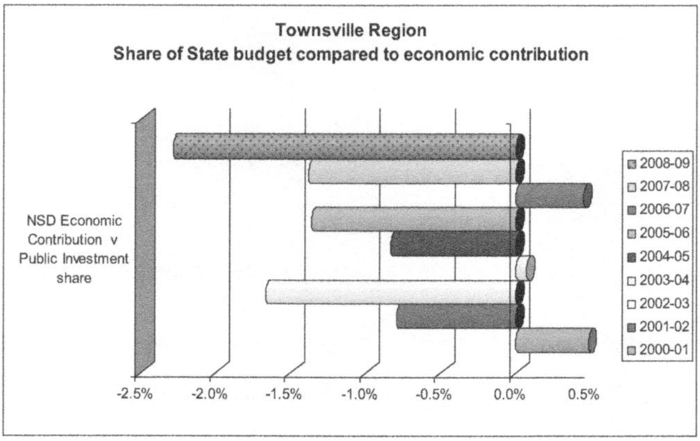

Source QLD Treasury, ABS DS Economics

In the nine budgets since 2000, the Townsville

region has been undervalued in an amazing 67% of previous state budgets.

Compounding this inequity, in four of those years the region was under-recognised by significant amounts. But, in the three years of positive recognition, the region only received less than 0.5% greater than their economic contribution. Positive recognition has not balanced the negative years.

Devastatingly, this year has seen the worst capital allocations to economic contribution since 2002, as the region lost out by almost $445m.

Contributing to this inequity is the state political monopoly that exists in Townsville. This is highlighted by each budget that has positively recognised Townsville's economic contribution, has only occurred in an election year.

A close inspection of the previous threes year's budgets reveals a narrowness in portfolio priorities, domination of regional servicing components and lack of economic capacity inclusions.

By 2008, the term Our Fair Share starts to appear more regularly in print, TV news and Radio media platforms. I was being interviewed by journalists from all over Queensland, in particular local Newspaper, TV and radio journalists, sometimes this occurred every second day. I eventually contributed almost one thousand comments and articles to Townsville Bulletin (source Tony Raggatt Townsville Bulletin Journalist) and possibly similar contribution in regional and Brisbane papers. Similarly there was an enormous contribution via TV news channels and radio interviews.

Following is an Editorial from the Townsville

Bulletin in 2008.

Townsville Bulletin
Saturday, August 9, 2008

Give the North its fair share

THOUGH hard political reality makes the call for North Queensland statehood a distant prospect at best, the sentiments behind the move are entirely understandable. The latest call comes on the back of research by economist Colin Dwyer, who said the northern region had contributed about $1 billion more than it had received over the past nine years. He said the North was being undervalued by the current State Government, compared to the contribution which the region receives in return. While this reasoning might

Our Fair Share

not be enough to gain much ground in the battle for the North to gain self-governance, it should add some weight to the belief that our region should be given a larger slice of the cake when it comes to funding. The even more convincing part of the equation for State treasury staff is that investing in our region should help to create even more revenue. The expansion and improvement of roads, rail corridors and other key parts of transport infrastructure is crucial to enabling the expansion of businesses of every kind. Whether it is allowing more efficient movement of minerals or the easy movement of tourists between destinations, the contribution of the State Government is vital to helping our economy maintain its growth. Ignoring the North in favour of the South-East corner simply makes no sense when there are great possibilities in various industries. Yet, as Mr Dwyer correctly points out, this is about more than money. Adequate and equal political representation compared to other states and territories seems nothing less than a right for residents of the North. Considering that our population is more than double the size of Tasmania, which has five members in the House of Representatives, our direct political influence seems poor. This is not to underestimate the hard work which our resident senators put in, or the ear-bending which they do on our behalf. Yet it is another cogent argument towards independence — and another reason why the State Government should be listening carefully.

Why does Our Fair Share matter?

Our Fair Share is about equity given economic and population contributions. It's about equity given comparative size and growth and it's about persuading voters, bureaucrats and politicians. Most of all it's a tool designed to help people.... in regional Australia.

If a regions population is growing strongly then it follows that it needs more services and different facilities. If it is growing strongly it is likely to be contributing above averagely to tax revenues. It follows that strongly growing regions need 'Our Fair Share' of public investment, at least at the level it is contributing, but possibly more, depending on its capacity to grow and contribute further revenue. If its growth is diminishing, then it possibly requires a targeted public investment strategy to assist with structural adjustment. If a region is stagnant and gets less than its fair share of public investment history shows that it struggles longer to recover and unemployment remains consistently unacceptable.

In the period 2002-2008 Townsville was booming, socially and economically. Its population growth was double the national average and well above the state average. Its economic growth was over 5% and consistently strong. Townsville social and economic advantage should have been high, but it wasn't, and as a consequence the region has strong growth but was underperforming.

These stronger than long run average conditions were driven by serval factors. Cashed up military personnel back from overseas deployments, a mining construction boom driven mostly by demand from Asia, a consequential residential construction boom, strong wages growth (5%/annum) and easier finances.

With strong economic and population growth appropriately strong public investment is needed to keep up with population and economic growth and change. Of course, there was strong competition for public finances. The federal government started running surpluses, but didn't share them equally with politically 'adversarial' states. There were layers to the political and economic Our Fair Share jigsaw and it needed a deep thinker to identify and quantify the challenges and develop simple solutions.

I wrote the following media information in 2008 and updated it in 2010:

State owes Townsville $1.4billion.

Recent research reveals that the state government in Brisbane owes the Townsville region $1.4billion. The research shows that state public investment in the region has consistently failed to meet expectations and has hampered sustainable progress. A sustainable community values diversity and strength in its economy just as it values diversity and strength in its social assets and environmental systems.

While local economic challenges and opportunities lie ahead the biggest challenge to overcome is to rectify a long term outstanding public investment debt from Brisbane.

Long term inconsistent State public investment continues to frustrate sustainable and fair economic growth in the Northern region. There are many levels of inconsistent state public investment in Townsville. The first inconsistency refers to how the money is spent, the second when it is spent, and the third how much is delivered.

For a long time between 2000 and 2010 state public investment was concentrated in a few large projects. For example, prisons expenditure was accelerated while new male, female and juvenile establishments where built at the opportunity cost of other significant community infrastructure. *It would be interesting to see the expenditure per prison cell in comparison to hospital beds?* While it is agreed that prisons expansion was required, the question remains at what cost to other important facilities that support Northern economic development and quality of life.

Elections (politics) played a big part in state public investment distributions and state public investment supports crucial facilities such as public hospitals, education facilities, energy provision and environmental maintenance. From 2000 to 2006 State public investment improvement was determined by election dates; when targeted and consistent public investment is known to achieve better outcomes for sustainable economic growth. Queensland Treasury data reveal that there has been increased capital spending before each State election; sometimes by as much as 1.8% of long-term investment. The community deserves better long term sustainable economic and social facility planning than this.

Unfortunately, and demonstrating poor economic planning, Townsville's economic contribution has been higher than state public investment. If the region received its economic contribution fair share of State public investment it would have received $281.7million more since 2005 and even more when we consider inflation.

Finally, the region accommodates a significant number of fly-in fly-out mine workers who depend on local public facilities and services and if we consider their economic contribution, the long-term state public investment underfund (Our Fair Share Debt) soars to $1.4billion- enough to expand our public hospital, improve our education facilities, build a sustainable baseload power station and build better roads for all northerners.

This very large Our Fair Share Debt reinforces the necessity to identify a better public investment distribution system. One that can identify social asset needs, qualify the net benefit of social facilities and deliver more consistent State public investment. One solution would be to consider recognition of the region's economic contribution, population growth and population share so local infrastructure adequately supports sustainable progress and improves our quality of lifestyle.

Fast forward to 2013/14 and Townsville economy is at the start of a prolonged downturn, which turns into a prolonged and deep recession and eventually a depression. It was driven by tight finance, APS and QPS staff cuts, a mining construction downturn, poor state public investment and tight financing arrangements; not getting Our Fair Share!. The media information demonstrates the broad use of Our Fair Share method during a time of different economic activity to the boom of 2002-2008.

"With Greater Townsville's unemployment at 8.4% (April 2014) and persistent, low business and consumer confidence and residential construction

below long run averages we need public capital injections, consistent public sector jobs and private sector innovation."

In capital expenditure terms, roads are our big winner followed by energy and water. My economic crystal ball can see more road works leading up to the next state election, which in my opinion wont be until after the G20 leaders meeting in Brisbane on November 15 & 16.

Disappointing parts of the state budget include local education investment, especially given the number of babies being born in the region and current comparative NAPLAN results. I am discouraged by the comments about sale of the port, frustrated with the lack of attention given to home insurance challenges for the 350,000 voters north of the Fitzroy and unsatisfied with the cost of living pressures being placed on pensioners.

Overall it was a solid state budget that reduces debt and deficits but was too optimistic about the doubling of economic growth to 6% next year. Greater Townsville and the rest of North Queensland deserves its Fair share of Public investment and has earned the right to consistent accuracy regarding the claims of politicians.

Our Fair Share has social, economic and political layers. Adding regions together develops stronger representation and possibly

satisfies several conditions for a new state. The use of Our Fair Share in aggregation demonstrates another level of application of the Our Fair Share method and provides a stronger political bargaining platform. It also provides original argument and evidence to deal with Brisdrain, and it actually strengthened the new state argument, that was previously anedoctal, emotional and arbitrary in its geographic definition. Even if a new state wasn't likely, Brisdrain and Cantberra certainly got the message that northerners weren't happy with current public investment allocations and were prepared to offer alternative solutions.

The following essay written in 2008, redefined the geographical boundaries of North Queensland, as a comparative jurisdiction. It is original information on geographic boundaries of North Queensland, economic population contribution and comparative political representation.

The essay demonstrates the geographically aggregated use of Our Fair Share, adding a vertical level to the term. It was becoming a complex, multi-layered, multifactorial persuasion term.

It highlighted that the public investment jigsaw couldn't just be solved by economics, a

feasibility study or a Cost Benefit Analysis; it also needed political influence.

Ultimately the argument became "give us Our Fair Share or we'll prosecute for a separate state." I needed to gather evidence and test this in a public forum, before committing to this path.

I was encouraged by a friend, several journalists and my own curiosity about contributions and share of public expenditures. My friend and I agreed that the initial commonly agreed definition of North Queensland was the Sarina line; it split the state in half. Unfortunately, when I looked at the numbers, I couldn't support such a division, there was not enough people, not enough economic activity and not enough political representation/influence to make it happen.

I completed the following research and put forward the suggestion that if there was to be a new state it needed to include Central Queensland (Fitzroy) and the Billions in revenue from agriculture and mining. I shared this information and it was quickly picked up by northern politicians.

Making the statement in the media at the time (2008) was difficult because the consequences were enormous for an economic consultant that relied on public sector for projects and income. But if I didn't make the statement, would the South be able to continue spending on projects in SEQ and not consider crucial projects for the North? I considered this and the risk of upsetting Brisbane for some time. I used decision matrices to remove emotion and other undesirable factors.

Eventually, I decided it needed to be said by someone different, articulate, local and someone with economic skills.

I said it first in the local paper. I repeated it on ABC local radio and I said it on TV news channels. I became the North Queensland economist. Would it make a difference for the people of North Australia's largest City* (*I first described this in 2008).

One thing became clear, the media liked it and constantly chased me for comment on every relevant story. There was some criticism by closed minded members of the community and some, mainly southern, politicians but when you're influencing change.... the establishment is always going to respond negatively and sometimes personally.

Existential North Queensland-an OFS essay I wrote in 2008

Recently, respected historian and academic Professor Geoffrey Blainey supported North Queensland becoming its own state. Rapid population growth has contributed to inadequate social and economic facilities right across the north and Blainey states that this country will look absurd if we have the same states in the future. Those who dare to dream and question the integrity of the current system, actually reveal a healthy, robust democracy that is willing to examine the integrity of the status quo and produce positive alternatives.

But, why should we continually revisit this concept and be so bold as to suggest progressive change?

The answer lies in 3 questions

1. Are we receiving fair representation in our national parliament?

2. Are we receiving fair reinvestment for our contribution to Queensland's prosperity?
3. Is there a cultural gap that separates North Queenslanders from our southern cousins?

When addressing these issues I will discuss state comparisons rather than individual indicators.

Defining North Queensland

North Queensland as defined by Associate Professor Philip Courtney is Rockhampton out west to the Territory border and north to Torres Strait. The commonly acknowledged definition of North Queensland is Sarina out west to the Territory border and north to Torres Strait.

Dwyers definition of North Queensland is closer to Courtneys, it includes the five statistical divisions Fitzroy, Northern, North West, Far North and Mackay. It also includes the local authorities in this zone. The reason Dwyer developed this new NQ region was to compile and compare valid and crucial data such as aggregated GRP, workforce and other economic, demographic and political information. The new NQ definition complied with standard ABS and OESR regions classifications. This was the first time North Queensland could validly compare itself to the residual of Queensland and other existing commonwealth jurisdictions.

North Queensland is a rising economic star.

It may be difficult to separate a historical link that has existed since before federation, but as parts of the North are continually being undervalued, there is a growing sentiment and evidence that in the future the north should be allowed to prosper independently and should prosecute the south and constitution in order to obtain a suitable outcome. Which poses a further challenge that of what is a suitable outcome?

State and Territory Comparisons

North Queensland's capabilities and contribution are highlighted by an interesting comparison between it and two other states and the northern territory. These states don't depend on South Queensland but they have enviable representation in Federal parliament and have a system of self determination.

An interesting basic geographic, demographic, political and economic comparison can be made between Tasmania, South Australia, Northern Territory and North Queensland. From a geographic perspective both Adelaide and Hobart are almost the same distance South and South West of Brisbane as Townsville is North of Brisbane. Neither state depends on south Queensland, but both have the ability to determine their own existence. Darwin is further away.

Tasmania

At the last census, Tasmania had the smallest population of any state in the commonwealth, of 495,000. It has a median age of 39 compared to Australia's of 37. Tasmania's economy is small and growing slowly, and in 2006 it contributed $19.6billion to GDP. Enviably, Tasmania has five members of the House of Representatives, and being a state, has a full voice in the Commonwealth's upper house with 12 senators and a seat at Federal state discussion tables such as COAG. There are solid benefits in having more federal representatives to argue for commonwealth public investment.

When we look at North Queensland it has almost double the population of Tasmania, at around 865,000 and its population is growing rapidly. The population is comparatively young.

Significantly, North Queensland's economy is growing rapidly, riding high on minerals and construction activity. North Queensland's economy contributes almost 2.5 times more than Tasmania does to Gross Domestic Product. According to QLD government experimental estimates, North Queensland contributed over $50billon to in 2006.

North Queensland has the same representation as Tasmania in the lower house of parliament but 83% or 10 fewer senators in the upper house. North Queensland is comparatively under-represented in federal matters. As we and members of all political parties in Townsville question the redistribution of Annandale and Wulguru to Mackay based Dawson electorate we reveal that Tasmania's five MP's are elected with an, on average, around 30% fewer voters, or around 20,000 voters less.

In 2006, North Queensland has 75% more population than Tasmania and its population is growing at a significantly faster rate. North Queensland contributed $30.5b more and is contributing at a significantly faster rate to Australia's economy than Tasmania.

Tasmania is a great place (though too cold) and just like North Queensland it has challenges, but Tasmania has the enviable ability to determine its own existence and future and has enviable federal political representation.

South Australia

When we compare North Queensland to South Australia we find similar results, although slightly different. In 2006, South Australia had a population of 1.57million which is growing at around 1% per annum; this is in comparison to around 2.2% for North Queensland. South Australia's economy is growing slowly (0.8%), and in 2006 it contributed $68.9billion to Australia's economy; 27% more than the North Queensland economy. But according to South Australia's Centre of Economic Studies the SA economy grew by only 0.8% in 2006.

OESR Research indicates the North Queensland

economy grew on average by 11.5% per annum between 2001 and 2006. Significantly, if this trend continues the North Queensland economy will overtake the South Australian economy by the end of 2009.

South Australia has ten members of the House of Representatives, and being a state, has a full voice in the Commonwealth's upper house with 12 senators and various other representations at federal discussions; once again comparatively more than North Queensland.

Interestingly, although subject to many variables, if population trends continue by 2036, North Queensland's population will be larger than South Australia's.

Northern Territory

When we compare North Queensland to the Northern Territory we find similar results, to Tasmania.

In 2006, NT had a population of 212,600 which is

growing at around 1.8% per annum since 2001; this is in comparison to around 2.2% for North Queensland. South Australia's economy was growing slowly (0.8%), and in 2006 it contributed $68.9billion to Australia's economy; 27% more than the North Queensland economy. But according to South Australia's Centre of Economic Studies the SA economy grew by only 0.8% in 2006.

OESR Research indicates the North Queensland economy grew on average by 11.5% per annum between 2001 and 2006. Significantly, if this trend continues the North Queensland economy will overtake the South Australian economy by the end of 2009.

South Australia has ten members of the House of Representatives, and being a state, has a full voice in the Commonwealth's upper house with 12 senators and various other representations at federal discussions; once again comparatively more than North Queensland.

Interestingly, although subject to many variables, if population trends continue by 2036, North Queensland's population will be larger than South Australia's.

Outcomes

Economically and population, North Queensland compares very favourably to many other Australian provinces. So maybe it is time to leave the family home, sit in the driver's seat and determine the direction we go.

NQ has a population larger than Tasmania and Northern Territory and an economy that dwarfs both Tasmania and Northern Territory and is snapping at the heels of South Australia. Yet North Queensland's federal representation is constrained by the current national and state political system. The North has taken the current system of representation for granted but, comparative economic evidence suggests its time to challenge the systems integrity. Indeed, a provincial comparative analysis reveals that North Queensland does not need South Queensland in order to prosper. As parts of the North are continually being undervalued via state public investment; self determination should be one of the North's intergenerational priorities.

When deciding which system you support, consider:

- Is North Queensland receiving fair reinvestment for our contribution to Queensland's prosperity?
- Is North Queensland receiving adequate compensation from Governments to compensate for the impact of the GFC.
- Is North Queensland receiving fair representation in our national parliament?
- Is there a cultural gap that separates North Queenslanders from our southern cousins?

Conclusion

Dwyer's new definition of NQ provides valid information to compare and contrast with other areas and existing jurisdictions. It provides significant initial information on how NQ might comply with section 124 of the constitution.

Blainey makes a positive contribution toward social and economic improvement for North Queensland, but realistically what choices do we have?

- Abolish the second tier of government and adopt a regional council of mayors.
- Establish a new state.
- Establish an upper house that in part represents regional and North Queensland.

However, maintaining the current system is surely the most likely and conservative outcome, but in my opinion, it may not be the best outcome for North Queensland.

What Professor Blainey was saying is the current centralised allocation and decision making system provides poor outcomes for isolated regions. It follows that for social and economic progress to occur, North Queensland needs a better system of representation and fairer share of public expenditure than it is currently receiving.

Those among us who argue that 'if it's not broken there's no need to fix it' should look at

1. Busiest health system in the State and possibly the country,
2. Consistently poor school education performances,
3. Inadequate Roads
4. Inadequate Rail
5. Inability to obtain necessary economic development infrastructures.
6. Lack of competitive power generation

as practical examples why we need a change for

the better.

If self determination was granted, North Queensland would generate its own revenue systems including GST revenue and the ability to spend it on region specific requirements. Significantly, revenue from our economic efforts would flow back into our own infrastructure needs and decisively we could determine our current and future contribution to Australian Society.

But, with any change comes benefits and challenges and, nobody suggests it will be easy, indeed there would be significant challenges, but from an economic, social and intergenerational perspective, it is much more preferable than the current system. Just like every other vibrant region in Australia, North Queensland needs to own their own economic, environmental, social and intergenerational destiny and not depend on centralised decisions from a parliament that is almost as far away from us as it is from Hobart or Adelaide.

Finally, if these other states can prosper amidst many challenges, then so too can an independent North Queensland. As the social and economic conditions continue to firm in the medium term, progressing our community as a sustainable entity can best be achieved by better federal representation, better quality state like representations and better allocations of North Queensland's current and future prosperity. See appendix 1 for Dwyer's New State Test

This essay gave Our Share Fair depth and structure. Depth because of the regional vertical integration involved in public investment and other finances. Structure because it created the opportunity to compare the whole region or parts thereof to other parts of Australia and even, internationally. It also added original layers, about aggregated economics and populations.

The essay includes original comparative political representation and representational equity, creating a new and original political technique to frame, wedge and influence decision makers.

This essay also provided better contemporary understanding of population, economic and representational shares. Importantly, It was easy enough for the general population to understand. It provides structure for

prosecuting a fair share of state public investment, quantifies the economic contribution and contemporary growth rates, comparative population sizes and growth and political representational equity.

Politics and Economics are ultimately about helping people; Our Fair Share gives regional people, important information they need to gain a political advantage over city decision makers.

Our Fair Share allows us to think deeply about simple, regional community needs.

3 PART TWO OUR FAIR SHARE COLUMNS

"Mr Dwyer has not only been fearless in his pursuit for improved regional infrastructure, but also fastidious.
His campaign demanding a "fair go" and for a better resourced and more liveable North Queensland has ensured regional voices and perspectives are heard across the state.
Through his work he has championed improvements on sections of the Bruce Highway, a decentralised public sector, fairer northern home insurance premiums and more.
This effort has no doubt created a stronger and more liveable North Queensland for all its residents."
Ashley Pilhoffer Journalist Mackay Mercury

INTRODUCTION

Part Two of this book is a collection of 74 Our Fair Share columns, classified into four frames of the Our Fair Share Campaign.

The Our Fair Share collection includes 34 Economics essays, 12 Tourism Development essays, 23 Political essays and five Population

and Social columns. There were ten columns classified as Miscellaneous and do not appear in this collection.

There is also a collection of over 100 other Our Fair Share articles that are not included in this book, but were published across various media channels.

I have added comments to each column to explain the reason behind its purpose.

Social elements and Population are fundamental variables in the Our Fair Share method. The size and growth of a city/region generally reflects the public investment it requires to service the needs of the people that live there. The location of various facilities is determined by size of local population and geographic connection with wider populations.

Our Fair Share has become an essential and easily understood tool in decision makers and influencers arsenal.

The Townsville Boab

The first column in this section is a story about how many residents come from other parts of Australia and overseas to live and thrive in Townsville. The paragraph "The South Townsville boab has survived in unfamiliar surroundings, far from home, confident and strong – a symbol of North Queensland resilience and a window into the future as we determine our destiny." Is a reflection of my own arrival in Townsville in 1983 to study at JCUNQ and go on to become an academic, respected regional economist and shrewd influencer.

Diverse roots feed strong community

ALMOST 30 years ago, Bob Hawke was strutting his stuff. Paul Keating swaggered and cussed. And South Townsville became part of the Better Cities program.

This program was designed to beautify tired, old suburbs into trendy, hip locations. Streets were transformed with trees. The back alleys, once dusty and potholed from dunny trucks and ice deliveries, were covered in smooth bitumen.

Down one alley, a mound of brown, sandy soil lay bare. It was the only mound without reticulated water.

Months earlier, my mother-in-law at the time had returned from an expedition to northwest Australia.

She had brought two boab seedlings back from thousands of kilometres away and given me two. She knew I wasn't a farmer, but I had promise as a gardener. Water was my community's and my challenge, so a boab was a perfect gift.

One seedling died under my mango tree but one survived and flourishes today. If you drive down Fifth Ave and take a left into Comet St, 10m down the dunny lane is the South Townsville boab tree, green and plump in wet season and naked and voluptuous in the dry.

The Better Cities program was Labor's way of rewarding its traditional supporters. Property values surged and the true believers prospered as young, urban professionals took advantage of an attractive and affordable suburb close to the CBD work zone and lifestyle facilities.

The South Townsville boab has survived in unfamiliar surroundings, far from home, confident and strong – a symbol of North Queensland resilience and a window into the future as we determine our destiny.

The South Townsville boab is part of the broad mix of inhabitants in our city and it's the variety in our inhabitants and the individual contribution they each make that makes us a strong, resilient community and economy.

The Boab tree stands tall and fat today, where it was planted.

Still Standing Strong - April 2020 the South Townsville Boab.

The following article takes a swipe at the facilities they have in south east Queensland and the number and standard of stadiums in North Queensland. It also reveals the variety of things to see and do in and around Townsville;

a common theme in my OFS Columns. My intent was to complement the lifestyle theme, an important element in people living and thriving in a regional location.

City basking in unique cultural glow – My Heacline Townsville Sparkles

HAPPY Tuesday and I'm so glad to see most of my readers were switched on last week and spotted the mistake. The Wallabies didn't play at the Gabba, they played at Suncorp. In my defence there are so many stadiums in the southeast corner. I apologise for mistaking the venue and would still like to hear from any of our six local state members about a comparatively fair funding deal for our proposed stadium.

On to other matters, what a fabulous variety of events Townsville region had on offer last weekend. Truly, a wonderful mix of art, Italian culture and sport; similar to any capital city but with a northern twist. Are we the capital of SportArt in regional Queensland?

On Friday evening I went for a walk along The Strand to see the Ephemera. It was the best version of this display in its history. It's still there this week so get down and enjoy this wonderful display. I particularly enjoyed the circular light display close to the Gregory St restaurant precinct. The sandcastles were the best I've ever seen.

Then on Saturday night the Cowboys played Canberra. What a crowd. Wouldn't surprise me if many Canberrans travelled to see this game and get warm. This was always the best time of year to escape Canberra because it gets down to minus 6 or worse. The Cowboys are a huge part of our culture. Let's hope they go all the way this year.

Ingham put on a great Italian festival over the weekend. This event has been part of our cultural heritage for ages. It's a celebration of individual culture and community tolerance. It's great we have such a diversity of cultures in our region.

To end off the weekend I enjoyed a Vivaldi concert in one of our older buildings with fantastic acoustics. Townsville can really sparkle when given the chance.

The variety and standard of events over the weekend really was world class.

While Townsville is the Sport & Cultural capital of regional Queensland, we need to complement that with value added options for visitors and locals. We need to drive home the positive lifestyle experience so visitors tell their friends about our unique northern culture.

Wouldn't it be great if we could consistently sparkle with public artworks along The Strand and up Castle Hill, develop unique lightshows and encourage creative buskers to Gregory Street?

When Townsville shines it really sparkles.

The Bigger Townsville concept is expected by most residents, especially at the time this Column was written. At the time of writing, there was a federal white paper on a larger national population but very little referred to about regions. I wrote this essay to influence decision makers to consider cities like Townsville in their population planning.

My reference to thought bubble election economics relates to my theory that seats and places like Townsville only get public investment recognition when an election comes around. I would argue that this might be good politics, but its poor economics and that consistent public investment is required to diversify a regional cities economy, jobs, population and boost resilience; resilience that would be tested in 2016 when QNI closed its doors and 800 high income workers lost their jobs.

I wrote at length about the relationship between political decisions and economic development inconsistency and the need for change. This is part of Our fair Share.

Townsville at half-a-million strong.

HAVE you considered what facilities a city of 200,000 people should have? What facilities does it have that need maintenance or upgrades?

What facilities would a regional city that could house 400,000 to 500,000 residents need over the next 40 years?

Last week the Federal Government released the fourth intergenerational report.

It forecast Australia's population to grow by 16 million within 40 years and the public facilities required to support this additional population could cost around $700 billion.

The Townsville region needs a smart plan to ensure we get our fair share of future public investment.

Thought-bubble economics each election won't cut through.

The Townsville region is a complex, vibrant location with spectacular environmental assets, unique social challenges and abundant economic opportunities. It is part of the complex web of cities that thrive in North Queensland.

If we include the northwest, it accounts for 1.3 per cent of the nation's economic activity and 1.1 per cent of its population.

Over the past decade, the region's population growth has been consistently higher than the national average. We need to work smarter to maintain this momentum.

If the Townsville region grows on average by 2 per cent per annum for the next 40 years, it will have a population of around half a million residents by 2055; two-and-a-half times larger than now and roughly the same size as Canberra and the Gold Coast at the moment.
What facilities do these locations have that we should be planning for? How many homes will we need and where will we put them?
What facilities does Townsville need now and what do we need to support a growing and much larger population? What facilities or services do you think Townsville needs now and over the next 40 years? Send me your ideas and I will include some of them in this column over the coming weeks.
Townsville needs to work smarter, and one way is to produce a regional infrastructure audit and cost-benefit ratio ranked community-needs analysis, so together we make a difference for current and future residents.
Thought-bubble projects, each election, should be a thing of the past.

In June 2014 I correctly forecast population changes that occur from that date forward. I also correctly forecast the economic downturn from 2014. My comment "We just need a smarter plan to even out the economic bumps." Is a way of saying regional horizontal fiscal equalization is a significant issue for Townsville. There are too many wide economic variations and not enough stability.

I go on to say "Many people would not remember the last time we had negative net migration and an underperforming economy. It was unpleasant."

My comparison to 1997 deep recession and population decline was rebuttal of Campbell Newman's State government staff cuts, a rejection of federal APS staff cuts and the consequences a similar 'foolish' strategy would have on Townsville almost 20 years later.

These poorly considered political decisions preordained his chances of winning the three local seats at the next election. As it turned out the LNP mustn't have read the column or if they did, they didn't understand it, because they lost all three seats by a landslide and power in Brisdrain.

Need to play smart or city will shrink
Words: 392

TOWNSVILLE is the largest city in North Australia and is expected to retain this title for the foreseeable future.
If Townsville maintains consistent population growth, it will achieve 200,000 residents sometime in the next 12 months.
However with consistently poor unemployment figures, higher than usual residential vacancy rates and some other challenging economic data,

Townsville could experience slower or even declining net migration.

We need to work smarter to attract our fair share of public and private job-creating and lifestyle-enhancing investment.

Regional population data for the year to June 2014 is released at the end of this month.

Population growth comprises net natural increase and net migration.

Net natural increase is the technical term for new babies minus the end of life experience. Our newborn numbers are likely to be positive and solid. Net migration is a crucial component of our population growth and is closely linked to jobs creation or decline, economic growth and confidence.

A variety of economic indicators are leading many economists to the conclusion that net migration could have slowed recently or it could be negative. It is unlikely to have grown.

We should not be surprised. This has happened in the past and will happen in the future.

We just need a smarter plan to even out the economic bumps.

Many people would not remember the last time we had negative net migration and an underperforming economy. It was unpleasant.

It doesn't look like our current leaders learnt much from that experience.

Townsville experienced negative net migration in 1997 and for a sustained period after that, Townsville's economy struggled.

Several factors contributed to the 1997 economic ditch including poor civic decisions, a politically complacent attitude towards our fair share of state and federal public expenditure and the 1996 Federal Government retrenchment program.
We will soon know our official population growth numbers but a combination of indicators leads to the conclusion that net migration in Townsville has slowed or declined.
Net natural increase has likely remained solid. Overall population growth is likely to have increased with our new babies leading the charge, but overall growth is likely to be lower than our long run average.
We need all levels of government to recognise our wider long-term economic, social and environmental contribution. We also need our leaders to plan a much smarter case for necessary job-creating and lifestyle-enhancing infrastructure.

Later in this column I use population evidence to encourage a strategic change from local decision makers. "Something better needs to be done to promote our region because our net migration is stumbling and our population growth and economy is restructuring."

I received criticism from significant decision makers. My insights and forecasts would eventually prove to be correct.

Time southerners got taste for region

Words: 466

BUDGET day is like grand final day for an economist. I like to buy pizza and beer, watch the Treasurer deliver economic tries and criticise the political referee's decisions. I've been doing this since I was in first year at James Cook University of North Queensland. Over the decades I've provided my budget opinion to national, state and local media sources for free. It's a way of promoting the value of my profession, encouraging public scrutiny of our tax dollars (keeping the bastards honest) and supporting my community.

I love Townsville and the lifestyle it offers. I want to be part of this great tropical city's future. As one of my professors used to say, scrutinise everything and offer better-informed solutions. There is enough evidence to suggest that our diversified economic challenges need a different, more positive approach. Something better needs to be done to promote our region because our net migration is stumbling and our population growth and economy is restructuring. Townsville's vision shouldn't be just about a one- dimensional CBD focus.

Recently I was in Melbourne and while relaxing I switched on the TV. I was saturated by State Labor Government adverts promoting regional Victoria's lifestyle and encouraging Melburnians to move to regional Victoria. While regional Victoria is waiting for a tsunami of southern city slickers, Townsville should be prosecuting for our fair share of long-term public investment, job creation and sustainable economic growth.

Victoria's population decentralisation policy is part of a similar silver buckshot approach required to promote and develop northern Queensland. Brisdrain whinges that it's overcrowded but I have little sympathy for an area that does nothing to promote southern residents moving to our regions.

When I worked in Cantberra, adverts of skimpily dressed healthy couples swimming in refreshing pools made me long for a tropical lifestyle. Townsville needs to advertise on southern television in the bitterly cold months to attract workers and families to our piece of warm sunny paradise. Townsville's brand sells itself; warm, inviting and tropically sunny. But if you don't tell them, they'll never know.

While our city's residents are having lots of babies and a solid net natural increase, we need to stop the leakage of some adults and families to southern locations. But we can't do it all on our own and we need tonight's Budget and state public investment to support a wider northern and northwest region that has contributed strongly over the past 150 years.

Remember, the three-year political cycle dictates government cut hard initially, consolidate in the second year and spend in the third year. After tonight's Budget I look forward to leftover pizza for breakfast and our region scoring some job-winning public investment. But it's not an election year so I hope the pizza tastes good served southern style: cold and wet.

My experienced and well researched forecasts were usually correct but on a few occasions they weren't. Some variables were out of my control, including technical recalibrations that couldn't be foreseen. Townsville is still waiting to achieve the 200,000 residents mark and in 2020, 200,000 residents is still a couple of years away.

Ostrich time's over for city hot spots

Words: 309

IN 2007 I revealed that Townsville was the largest city in North Australia and, as previously revealed in this column, Townsville is set to crack the 200,000 population mark in late 2015.

Here's another forecast: given consistent population growth, in 20 years, Townsville will be the 11th largest city in Australia, have a population over 300,000 and leapfrog Geelong and Hobart.

Governments can't ostrich out and pretend we don't exist. They need to provide Townsville with our fair share of public investment, and also monitor and act on city areas that are driving population and construction growth so the quality of life of residents is not diminished.

Townsville is growing at an above-average rate. The estimated growth for the city was 2.5 per cent.

The nation grew by 1.8 per cent and the state by 1.9 per cent. DS Economics estimates for Townsville's April 2014 population is likely to be around 192,644; given steady population growth.

In 2012-13 Townsville City was the largest and fastest-growing major city in North Queensland. But population growth wasn't consistent across Townsville; indeed we have a national population hotspot.

In the year to June 2013 Deeragun had the fastest population growth in Townsville, increasing by 8.9 per cent, almost five times the national and state average. Deeragun is unsurprisingly a residential construction hotspot with 641 dwellings being approved in the year to January 2014. Deeragun accounts for 32 per cent of population growth and 40 per cent of residential construction In Townsville.

Over the next 20 years Deeragun and Cosgrove will play a strong part in housing Townsville's anticipated 110,000 additional residents. It's likely that by 2025 this wider Northern Beaches location will construct over 10,000 new dwellings and house over 25,000 new residents. These suburbs need "our fair share" of public investment and services so residents' tropical lifestyle is consistent with national benchmarks.

Take a look at those home approvals in Deeragun!! In 2013 it was a state population growth hotspot but by 2016 it was struggling. After QNI closure Deeragun median home

prices had plummeted and residents were struggling to pay their mortgages. Job security was a challenge and people were leaving town to find work. Townsville was experiencing a recession between 2013-15 but with the closure of QNI it had become a localized depression. Calls for Our Fair Share of public investment curiously went underfunded in 2016 state budget. This budget occurred before the federal election in 2016 and the state was maybe hoping for a federal political wedging match to pull Townsville out, rather than invest themselves. The Stadium is an example of this. The Labor state government "passively offered" $100m but only if the Federal government committed $150m to the project. The state probably thought it didn't have to spend the money on a seemingly uneconomic facility of low importance. But it would look good if it offered – classic regional wedge politics. But elections have a way of changing economic decisions and expenditure. I was a candidate in this federal election. Six weeks out from election day and the polls had the liberal incumbent wining with a healthy margin. The incumbent didn't need preferences, so he attacked me at every public opportunity.

I ran an evidence based strategy, ignoring his bewildering strategy. I regularly pointed out the economic mess that Townsville was in. Indeed, the construction industry was in a massive

downturn and something needed to change. The sitting member was part of the challenge not solution.
Two weeks out from election day and a representative of the incumbent contacted me to seek my preferences. Amused, I pointed out that this could not happen because the 'How to vote forms' were submitted at time of nomination!!

This was still an opportunity for Townsville; I agreed to support the economic platform of the incumbent if asked, and only if the agreement was ratified such that if the sitting member lost and the Liberals won, they would stick to the funding agreement. Importantly, I protected this agreement by arranging with the editor of the Townsville Bulletin, to print their support, so it was on the public record.

Its not widely known that I played a crucial but small role in funding for the new Townsville Stadium, politics had usurped economics and Our Fair Share had proved a useful tool in securing regional and pivotal Public Investment.

Tourism Columns

Tourism has been a contentious issue in Townsville for decades. Townsville was originally the location of the only international airport in North Queensland. This was because of Townsville's central location to Cairns, Whitsundays and Outback. I remember my as a child, family was in Sydney in 1969. We were travelling back to PNG and wanted to stop off along the way. The only option offered to my parents was Townsville and Magnetic Island. This 'product offer' changed within a decade. By the 1980s the airport had been transferred to Cairns. This saw Townsville struggle to gain a better share of the worlds fastest growing industry. In the 1990's most regional economists were providing public advice for Townsville to gain a better share of Tourism to boost their economy and gain better access to public investment.

My Tourism columns raise the local tourism profile but they also serve to challenge the existing stagnant strategy and raise other opportunities like Adventure and Cultural Tourism.

In the following column I recall two natural events that when combined, create a Wildlife special. I highlight an underutilised

environmental asset that with clever investment could create a greater share of tourist arriving in Townsville. This was my second Column and first on Tourism. In total I wrote 12 unique tourism columns. Tourism was not my key focus. The key purpose of Our Fair Share is still better public Investment and improved representation shares in Cantberra and Brisdrain.

Termite invasion a sight to behold

Words: 297

THE Friday evening after Cyclone Dylan there was a mass spawning of flying termites. They were everywhere!

As I was driving home, about 7pm, there were millions of the buggers crunching into the lights of my car and filling the evening sky. It was amazing. The road and sky was literally filled with these critters. The darkness would have saved many from being eaten but many animals including Cane Toads, birds and bats where feasting on the swarm. It was like a terrestrial coral spawning.

I'm guessing the recent rain, temperature and light winds after the cyclone triggered this mass swarm. I have seen this event in Townsville but not for a long time and never on this scale. Who needs

David Attenborough and a TV when ‘wildlife’ is happening in your backyard.
Townsville sure has its fair share of wonderful and nasty events such as cyclones in rainforests, reef spawnings and termite spawnings.
Our region is an environmental masterpiece that should be shared with the world.
Our part of the world is unique. To our north we have World Heritage-listed rainforest and waterfalls of Paluma. To our east lies the Great Barrier Reef. To our west are desert plains and upland rivers. But just south is a little-known jewel, a Ramsar-listed wetland called Bowling Green Bay. Part of this vast wetlands system is called Cromarty. Although I have never visited Cromarty I have read that this place contains more biodiversity than Kakadu and, as the season changes from wet to dry, it has more variety throughout the year.
Developing a low-impact tourism facility in this location would attract more tourists to Townsville to experience the variety of wildlife and environmental events that occur in our backyard and help to attract our fair share of international tourists.

The following two columns are Tourism related and keep in Frame with the Our Fair Share strategy. They were designed to be both funny and economics based. These columns received the many positive responses from readers, such as you’re becoming a very professional columnist. They were light hearted, evidence based and uncontentious. They were part of a

lead up to an anticipated change; a greater focus on Public Investment shares. They were written in early 2013.

Romanceville

I thought, for Valentine's Day, I'd write something on the economics of romance. So I Googled "economics of romance" and got a low cost dating website. The process was quick but unsatisfying. I needed to search for a deeper understanding of how romance impacts our local economy and if we are getting our fair share.

Townsville is a unique opportunity for romantics but it has some interesting challenges. If surfing the net or trolling Facebook is not your idea of romantic interaction then a little demographic knowledge may help you find that special person.

Firstly we have precincts in our city where there is significantly more of one gender than the other. If you're a young man seeking intelligent conversation think tertiary education. James Cook University and Barrier Reef TAFE have far more female students than male students; in one case there are 2 females for every male student. If you're an older man then those locations both have far more female staff than male staff.

If you are female there are multiple opportunities. If you are interested in the ruggedly handsome macho type then Townsville is home to the largest army base in Australia, which has a male dominated workforce. Then again the suburb of Stuart pops up as a male dominated suburb on the census and if you don't mind a man with a dubious past then maybe this location is a good starting point for you. At least you know he won't be leaving town for some time.

But seriously romance runs the economy. This Friday, Townsville restaurants & cafes will be filled with lovers and flirters. After a solid Christmas season local restaurants & cafes will do more than solid trade. Flower shops will have their busiest day of the year. Bottle shops and pubs will be selling more than usual quantities of wine. Taxis' should be busier than normal. Romance supports so many local jobs and businesses.

I hope we all get our fair share of romance on Friday.

Ready to dethrone Paris for lovers

Words: 343

THERE was such a great response to the recent romanceville article that I thought I would entertain you with some extra information and bold claims.

Townsville can be the romance capital of the Pacific. But we need to understand our romantic strengths and challenges. We've got a lot to offer and we're far sexier than any other Australian or Pacific city.

Like Paris or Rome, Townsville can be one of the great romantic destinations. Not because we have brilliant architecture or fantastic wine but because of the splendid isolation, consistent sunshine and unique food experience. The challenge is very few international travellers know about our romantic assets. We need to reveal our budgie smugglers and raise the skirt to attract more interest in our region.

So to start the ball rolling, have you ever visited the Boiling Pot south of Townsville? Chances are you've never even heard of it but it's spectacular during wet season. There's a waterfall in the shape of a love heart. The location is reasonably isolated and usually there's nobody there. You and your lover can experience natural North Queensland isolation.

There are so many other romantic locations around the Romance capital of the Pacific, like snorkelling in Arthur Bay, sunset cuddles at West Point and skinny dipping at Rollingstone Creek _ all isolated and extremely romantic.

Combine Townsville's romantic locations with the fresh food and Townsville is sexy. The fresh coral trout and nanagai from Cleveland Bay is the best I've eaten and Townsville crabs are some of the best you'll get.

Townsville also has a comparatively educated and good looking group of residents. All healthy assets on any romance index.
Townsville can compete as a major romantic destination. The type of city where the activity tires you out, the food is fantastic and the isolated natural experience is unique and memorable. So take your lover to the Boiling Pot soon and you'll see what I mean.
Townsville sure has its fair share of dead sexy assets which we are happy to share safely with any romantic travellers.

By this stage the Column had gained a good following that people were phoning the Bulletin asking where the Boiling Pot was and how to get there. People were asking if I knew of any other locations to visit. They loved the cheeky references to romance, but this was all about to change. The economic and political messages were more important than the demographic one.

The next article was a collection of places tourists and locals could visit around Townsville. It gently raises the issue of branding of Townsville. In 2006 I wrote an article about Australia's Mediterranean – Townsville. It was a property based story and the media loved it. This was a recollection of

that branding and a lead into other reputation based columns.

Time to share North's natural gems
Words: 390

NORTH Australia's largest city, Townsville, has a host of wonderful places to visit. Locals know about these destinations and it's time we shared them with the world. Here are five of my favourite drives in The Australian Mediterranean.

Castle Hill

Australia's second largest monolith captures some of the best driving views in Australia. These views define the largest city in North Australia. Northern views over the Coral Sea to Magnetic Island are stunning. Western evening vistas offer impressive sunsets and easterly sunrises are awesome. Finish with a coffee at Sweet Bridge Larder for a great view.

Hinchinbrook

Past Ingham through cane fields and remnant rainforest is a steep incline. Once you reach the top, this location offers incredible views of Hinchinbrook Island and her calm channel. Hinchinbrook is the largest island on the Great Barrier Reef and largest national park island in Australia. The rainforest-crusted island complements the wonderful mosaic of creeks and mangroves. This view is breathtaking. On the return journey consider stocking up with authentic Italian products and local produce at Lou's deli in Ingham.

Paluma

Drive just north of Townsville to discover the southern tip of the world heritage listed rainforest. A windy road takes you to little Crystal Creek Bridge and a spectacular swimming hole. Listen out for the cassowaries making their guttural mating call. On the way home stop off for the best mango gelato in Australia at Frosty Mango.

The Strand

This drive is short but well worth it. The best esplanade in Australia has great beaches and welcoming parks. Stop at Odyssey on The Strand for a taste of Townsville. Combine this with a drive to Pallarenda and it's my favourite short drive in the Australian Mediterranean.

Picnic to Horseshoe Bay

In September the kapok trees bloom with golden flowers. They dot the undulating landscape of our northern jewel. As you leave Picnic Bay stop at the parking area overlooking Rocky Bay for some romantic glimpses. Then wind your way past Arcadia over the hill to the frangipani-lined streets of Horseshoe Bay and enjoy lunch at the Horseshoe Bay pub while looking at the moored yachts.

Townsville is a special place, a leading city in regional Australia, with a stunning environment, Mediterranean type dry sunny climate and growing reputation as the largest city in North Australia. There's much more where this came from.

Building the frame that Townsville needed a better Brand, I retell a survivor type story from my youth in the next column. A story that introduces a new concept for Townsville Tourism reputation, Adventure Tourism. If Townsville was to capture a better share of international tourism it needed to diversify and subbrand. I finish with "A tropical island survivor experience would enhance our reputation as an adventure tourism destination and ensure we get our share of the adventure tourism market." Im still on frame and wedging the establishment with some alternative suggestions.

Islands can host adventure tourism
Words: 410

TOWNSVILLE has several isolated and spectacular islands on its doorstep.
These gems and their surrounding waters offer abundant adventure opportunities to challenge us and future generations. Have you ever taken yourself out of your comfort zone to test if you can live a subsistence lifestyle?
The risk is high but the rewards are great. I have travelled to several such tropical islands, endured

hardship and survived, returning with a stronger character and greater passion for our region and its environment.

One tropical survivor trip involved a small group. We travelled to a remote island in a half-cabin speedboat. While the others packed food for five days, I took nothing but water, a knife, towel and a fishing line. The first night I helped set up camp and used my towel as a pillow. I caught some small fish and cooked them on an open fire for dinner. Bush tucker at its best.

The next morning I rose early to witness a swarm of exquisite tropical butterflies crossing the Coral Sea. I set off for the other side of the island to test life and my survivor abilities. I scrambled over rocks and climbed steep hills until I spied what I was after, a herd of feral goats. I established camp and set about catching the smallest kid. But the kid was far more nimble than I and easily escaped my ineffective attempts to catch it. That night I went hungry, and was woken several times by rain and inquisitive small wild beasts.

I awoke ravenous and sleep deprived. I collected periwinkles and used them to catch fish. With no fire I enjoyed a nourishing meal of sashimi and started my journey back to camp where my fellow travellers were relieved to see me.

For five days, I lived on shellfish, fresh fish and water. I did more than survive. I may have lost weight and been sleep deprived but I gained passion, respect and a wonderful memory. I learned to respect animals more, contribute to a team and survive on a tough but gorgeous Tropical Island.

Bear Grylls has popularised survivor experiences with his TV shows. Millions over the world watch them. Before him, was our very own Bush Tuckerman Les Hiddins.

Townsville should leverage off these shows with tourism adventures on our uninhabited islands. A tropical island survivor experience would enhance our reputation as an adventure tourism destination and ensure we get our share of the adventure tourism market.

In 2013 a representative from the US embassy came to Townsville. The Chamber referred him to me. He told me that China would be the biggest tourism opportunity over the next decade. This column is on frame encouraging decision makers to think big and build opportunity through diversity.

In 2013 I met the Vice Premier of a State in China who was interested in developing closer ties with Townsville. It was an opportunity that was eventually lost by Townsville decision makers.

Spread the riches with more events

Words: 358

WHAT a bonza five months it's been for festivals and events in the largest city in North Australia.
These events happen because of our generous and hardworking volunteers, in all our sporting and cultural organisations.
Townsville sporting and cultural organisations need better fiscal recognition than they have received in the past and we also need a bolder vision that diversifies the timing of new events.
Our grassroots sporting and cultural organisations are fantastic and the events they have organised have been wonderful.
These events supported hundreds, maybe thousands, of indirect Townsville jobs in many industries.
Visitors filtered into the largest city in North Australia to enjoy sunshine, sea, spectacular sunsets and festivals.
Townsville sporting and cultural organisations need to be congratulated for contributing a significant economic injection into the local economy.
These organisations donate their time to run these successful events and deserve the community's admiration, corporate financial gratitude and public sector fiscal support.
Townsville is the events capital of North Queensland but it can't rest on these past achievements.
Townsville needs to capitalise on these unique economic drivers to achieve maximum potential.
Townsville can expand on this boutique national, sub state and state level events if these

organisations get our support and co-ordinate their efforts.

Our cool dry season presents ideal opportunities for talented people to perform and enjoy our part of Austra-utopia.

One international opportunity is Chinese New Year.

Chinese New Year is celebrated by billions of people around the world and it provides a unique opportunity for cultural and economic ties to develop between China and Townsville. Chinese New Year is usually held at the end of January to early February.

If we could entice a Chinese province to bring circus, culinary events, fireworks and Chinese opera performers it could boost our international festival opportunities, diversify our seasonal tourism industry and, who knows, maybe encourage economic and international education ties between our two countries.

Well done Townsville sports and cultural organisations, your performers and competitors. Your supporters are welcome back anytime.

Let's get behind our great sporting and cultural organisations, capitalise on future events and festivals opportunities and diversify our fair share of events tourism.

This next tourism based column promotes local lateral thinking in a competitive international tourism market. I encourage the reader to Think BIG like The Strand redevelopment, offer a new opportunity in a glass bottom walkway

on Castle Hill and develop the frame of our fair share and diversification. I received criticism for this column some people thought it was deviating from the plan, some thought the cost of a bridge would be too high. Imagine if Townsville had such a bridge now!

Hill could unwrap 'out of box' tourism
Words: 400

WHEN I arrived in Townsville more than 30 years ago, The Strand was a tourism disaster zone. Along most of this now iconic precinct was a 2m-high rock wall, infected with feral cats and other vermin. Cyclones are a fact of life in the North. The council of the time decided to protect The Strand and riparian zone with huge granite boulders. Ugly, smelly and it smacked of a knee-jerk reaction and fear of cyclones.

Before 1998 Townsville's famous Strand was the product of lilapsophobian town planning and simple silver bullet community disaster management. The Strand is now Townsville's primary recreation facility where tourists return to each time they visit the northern adventure capital, to enjoy the views.

Townsville and The Strand's new welcome mat reads beautiful, innovative and adventurous city. The view from The Strand last week of a squadron of spinnakers competing in the Maggie Island race week was spectacular, the kite surfers were

fantastic and the sabots screaming along the Strand all made up a wonderful festival of wind.
This distinctive festival owes part of its success to the vision and courage that recreated The Strand.
But Townsville can't rest on its past achievements. We need new ideas and new pathways to capitalise on our comparative advantages. I like the concept of a young adults' water park on the Strand or Rose Bay and the walkway from the proposed new coliseum that links the Strand to our multiple recreational places.
But this is traditional keeping up with the southern neighbours' development that's not really going to change our reputation.
Townsville needs ideas that burst outside the box and complement our Adventure city status. So here's another suggestion that is a massive success in the Grand Canyon. It's a skywalk similar to the structure in the Grand Canyon West, built out from the top of Castle Hill. It would be cyclone proof and have reinforced glass floor that would give each tourist the thrill to complement shark cage diving, crocodile cage diving, snorkelling with whales and any acrophobia they may have. Add to this, local produce with regionally distinctive dishes in our quality restaurants and we have a change wave driver in tourism for Townsville. It's not the silver bullet approach that develops reputations; tourists want multiple experiences and they will stay longer, tell their friends about Townsville so our reputation develops, endures and innovates ahead of competitors.

In 2014 Townsville was losing jobs. Its peak bodies thought the answer was tourism, but conventional tourism. I thought tourism was part of the solution but should not be emphasized as much, because it generally has lower paying low skilled roles. I thought a diversified plan was a better option. I also believed Townsville region needed a plan to attract conventional tourism but also a bigger diversified tourism sub plan to develop the next opportunity and the next market. Leveraging off an existing festival and growing the tourism market in off season was rejected by decision makers.

Opera festival could heat up tropics

Words: 389

AUSTRALIA'S leading tropical university is named after a bold explorer who took calculated risks. In the late 1990s James Cook University of North Queensland almost went bust. An aggressive expansion policy complemented by a bold community engagement vision saw the tropical university struggle financially.

During the university's tumultuous 1990s, campuses opened in Cairns, Mackay followed by the highly successful Singapore. If we look back on these fiscally turbulent times for our university we acknowledge a bold vision that has been realised in many ways including the community contribution made to Townsville by establishing the Australian Festival of Chamber Music.

This festival has emerged as a pinnacle event on the world music calendar. Performers from all over the world visit Townsville in the cool dry season to sample tropical lifestyles and perform. The AFCM does so much more for Townsville than attracting world's best performers from Russia, Holland, UK and America – it attracts audiences from all over the country and planet.

Most of these spectators are friendly, high net-wealth individuals with a vast network of traditional and Facebook friends. They revel in the balmy tropical climate while it is freezing cold down south and tell their friends about the fantastic events and glorious northern city of Townsville.

This year's new Sunday evening Concert Crawl was refreshing. The mainly southern audience of around 400 moved between three venues, were entertained by charismatic performers, amazed by the comparatively warm weather and amused by welcoming locals. By now these patrons would know about Maggie Island, whales, Castle Hill and The Strand. They have sampled tropical lifestyle.

This baby boomer market is only going to get bigger; they have money and an appetite for unique

events like the Sydney Opera on the Harbour. A tropical opera festival at Jezzine barracks over the October long weekend celebrating the end to the "cool dry" would cement our reputation as the classical music centre of the tropics. The Strand Ephemera and Shakespeare in the Park could complement it.
If the university and Ray Golding had not had the guts to take a risk with the AFCM 20 or so years ago, Townsville would be the poorer now. Again Townsville seeks a bold organisation or organisations that will take a chance on a new festival, boost our reputation and contribute to the future diversity of the North.

I wrote about action and adventure, while trying to convince decision makers that if tourism is the goal, Townsville needs a diverse portfolio of tour opportunities to attract and retain tourists. Our Fair Share is about adventure, diversity and endurance. In this OFS essay I raise concern for the economy with the important statement "Now is the time for business to innovate, for governments to facilitate and for everyone to think outside the box." I had received push back from decision makers with this well sourced and considered evidence. My conclusions would eventually come true.

Let's relaunch as Australia's Adventure Capital
Words: 373

LAST year I went swimming with beautiful great white sharks in the great southern ocean. I travelled the length of the country to Port Lincoln in South Australia for my 50th birthday.

The shark experience was awesome and the food fantastic, with fresh tuna sashimi, local Coffin Bay oysters and crisp sparkling wines from neighbouring Boston Bay. I couldn't get enough.

Travellers of all ages spend big money on these wildlife, foodie adventure experiences. The boat was full of international tourists and Australians on a bucket list binge.

This is our opportunity to rebrand tourism in Townsville and add a different dimension to our economy. Our back yard is full of these experiences, many of which I have tasted but unfortunately some are difficult to arrange. There's one item I need to tick off my bucket list. Whales off Magnetic Island.

July/August is migration season for these east coast giants. I've been told the best way to see them is on a jet ski. So, in August on a fine day, I'm going to don the wetsuit and treat myself to this special experience: Adventure City whale watching.

Townsville has many other underused environmental assets that we can capitalise on such as sharks, crocodiles and unique food experiences. There's no doubt that our tourism sector needs a makeover; rather than the titles of Garrison City or antonym for dead boring, alive with curiosity, we need to rebrand Townsville as the

Adventure Capital of Australia. We can do this, and the net benefit will be handsome.

Imagine being able to wild shark cage dive one day, the next day experience the ferocity of a wild North Queensland crocodile, followed by an up-close experience with the gentle giants of the Coral Sea, migrating whales, all complemented by local fresh produce in our restaurants. It would be electric, infectious and enduring.

Tourists would stay longer, spend more and tell others about our great attractions.

Townsville and its people have so much going for us. Now is the time for business to innovate, for governments to facilitate and for everyone to think outside the box.

So which quest will you complete in the Adventure Capital of Australia this year – Sunshine, Sunsets, Sharks, Sashimi and Sparkling Smiles?

The next article is on theme, inspiring lateral thinking and encouraging the establishment of a new tourism asset that would be unique to Townsville in Queensland. I think Hemingway would have liked this essay.

Sharks, crocs improve island appeal

Words: 399

MAGNETIC Island used to be the jewel in our tourism crown, but it's become another residential location.

Since the development of The Strand do locals visit the island as often? How can we boost the profile of this tourism diamond so it compliments our region's lifestyle, sustainability and economic growth?

The reason why I visit the island is simple – it's a gorgeous place.

Recently I walked from Horseshoe to Balding Bay for the first time. I discovered a breathtakingly beautiful and isolated bay. I also went to West Point.

Romantics need venture no further than this island to achieve perfect isolation with stimulating natural beauty.

I love to snorkel, dive and do all the adventure activities our region has to offer. When the Magnetic Coast gets those still, warm days and calm seas the sediment in the bay drops and visibility in the Coral Sea improves there are several patches of coral around the island that are the best, most accessible reef to snorkel or dive, anywhere in the North.

Incidentally, while I was preparing to snorkel on the Xbase reef, I noticed a full bus arriving. I counted 51 adventurers disembarking. After considering the gender of the busload of backpackers I realised that there were four females for every male. As if young blokes didn't already have a reason to explore Magnetic Island?

Anyway, I swam over to the patch of reef and enjoyed a brilliant afternoon of snorkelling. Although the beauty of this small patch of reef has dwindled over the past nine years I saw five giant clams, schools of fish and interesting bombes and coral.

There are so many reasons to visit Magnetic Island but since the aforementioned development in Townsville the island has slipped as a tourism magnet.

While there are baseloads of sunshine, ample secluded beaches, convenient access to ruggedly handsome bays and romantic champagne sunsets that would entice anybody, "Maggie" just seems to lack a niche or the right mix of combined points of difference.

Our abundance of beautiful sharks and captivating crocodiles might be part of the solution. Darwin has popular crocodile cage diving for $160 a go and Port Lincoln has world famous shark cage diving for $500 a trip. Maybe the $5 billion Northern Development Fund could help us with a feasibility study that boosts the educational eco-tourism profile of Magnetic Island with crocodile and shark cage diving?

For many years public investment in Townsville took the form of youth prisons and block buildings – see my 'capital punishment' article above. Name one building in Townsville that is architecturally significant, so significant that it attracts visitors to see just that building? Prior to 2020 no such building existed. I point this out in this article and once again suggest a diversification of public investment. I

contribute significant Intellectual Property in some of these columns.

Starring role for a new arts centre

Words: 428

I'M colourblind, you know, I fail the dot test. So it's hard to have a credible opinion on matching colour schemes. I've learnt to cope. Townsville has also learned to cope with its one high-rise building on The Strand, which incidentally is now 45 years old. It's Townsville's best effort at having a unique building, something to look at when you fly over Townsville. In my humble, colourblind opinion, the new paint job looks like a mercurial Brisdrain Roar soccer fan rather than a tropical masterpiece. Anyway the building is there and it is what it is, but we can do better.

There are two places I enjoy flying into: Sydney and Port Moresby. Each is unique but they have one thing in common – the architecture is fascinating.

As you fly into Port Moresby (Townsville's closest capital city), you pass over tropical settlements scattered over hills, sea and plains. The architecture is unique with the most interesting example being PNG's Parliament House. Strong and powerful, this building stands as the best example of tropical design in the world. While I'm not suggesting we adopt PNG's building codes,

Townsville can learn from our close tropical neighbour about attractive buildings.
We should also learn from Australia's prettiest city to fly in to – Sydney. While it may rob our Cowboys of NRL glory each year, Sydney sparkles with its unique waterfront architecture. The iconic Harbour Bridge and Opera House are symbols of a young nation proudly displaying its ingenuity and innovation.
Townsville needs leadership and vision, and support from local, federal and state governments to create an iconic building – one that fascinates visitors and expresses our emotions. Jezzine Barracks could be the ideal place to locate an iconic tropical building. One suggestion put forward for the community needs register I canvassed two weeks ago is a new performing arts centre for Townsville.
How about a tropical-designed performing and visual arts space, as iconic as the Sydney Opera House and as Australian as the Southern Cross. Imagine a uniquely constructed and cyclone-proof complex of six geodesic domes in the form of this iconic southern constellation and illuminated at night. The largest dome would have eight arms, one more than the current Federation Star. As planes arrive and depart from Townsville airport, passengers would marvel at this cultural symbol of our city.
A unique tropical performing arts building is an innovative way of strengthening our distinctive lifestyle – another piece in the puzzle to achieve

our fair share of public and private investment, capitalise on our strengths and create jobs.

Townsville is not on the national radar. But its interesting to highlight some of the unique things Townsville contributes to the nation.

Region punches well above its weight
Words: 343

THE Magnetic Coast (Townsville Region) is not just an economic powerhouse of the north with loads of potential; she also has a unique and attractive lifestyle.
Her sporting teams have dominated the country, her cultural events dazzled the nation and her environmental assets are internationally renowned.
She blends a distinctive style with her desirable qualities and unique achievements that are unlike any other.
Amazingly, Magnetic Coast is home to four national sporting teams. Our sporting success in women's national basketball is remarkable; our success in a variety of other codes is looming and will build our reputation as the sporting capital of North Queensland. The NQ Cowboys have been promising to deliver to their full potential for many years and no Sydney referee is going to deny us NRL glory in 2015.

Townsville's previous success hosting big game events reinforces our ability to attract future national and international events.

Who could forget the British Lions match in 2000 followed by the 2003 Rugby World Cup and T20 match between Queensland and Victoria? Our sporting facilities if upgraded could host international T20 matches and AFL games. Imagine a triple header weekend, of T20, AFL and Super 15.

Arguably, our arts and culture season is the best in North Australia with the Festival of Chamber Music, Savannah Literary Festival and a variety of other cultural festivals.

Our performing arts facilities are solidly booked for months but if a planned refurbishment of the Civic Theatre in 2018 occurs, there will be no quality theatre for use in Townsville for six months.

Environmentally Townsville has excellent access to many internationally acclaimed natural wonders, including the southern end of world heritage rainforest at Paluma and the accessible coral reef snorkelling grounds off Magnetic Island.

To our south are the magnificent RAMSAR-listed wetlands of Bowling Green Bay with upper wet season waterfalls and downstream significant biodiversity wetlands of the Cromarty.

If you prefer sunshine to rain, then she can turn it on, 300 days a year. Magnetic Coast is a cracker of a place to live work and play.

Political Columns

A big part of Our Fair Share is the art of persuasion and these politically framed columns are shrewd and humorous. Politics in Townsville is very adversarial. If you stand up, there's always someone willing to try and pull you back, unfortunately it sometimes gets personal.

For a long time comments in the paper about any candidate from any political party were attacked by opposing parties. A metaphor might help understand my position here; im kicking a penalty. As I place the ball, a lone voice in the crowd yells out "You've got white hair" another yells, "You're an old bugger". As I approach the ball a chorus of opposition voices drown out the silent supportive section of the crowd.
I wouldn't stop before the ball and submit to the negative comments; would you?
I always kicked that ball with strength, determination and articulation. If I'd stop and look, the negative strategy would have won and they aren't even part of the game!!

My strategy was to prepare for the moment so I did the best I could, ignore the negativity and concentrate on the task.

This excerpt from a column adds humor in a clever way to the aggressive armchair distraction – regional politics.
"Fellow mangos, blueberries, strawberries, bananas, apples and watermelons, let's share a smile. The Tories have a hilarious name for the Greens. They've nicknamed them Watermelons. Watermelons are green on the outside and red on the inside. Politics can be hard for the communally sensitive, but a clever jibe can be a friendly way to get your message across."

The following was Our Fair Shares first column. It was published on Australia Day 2013.

BEING AUSTRALIAN 26 January 2013

As Australia Day approaches its appropriate to consider what it is that makes us Australian? Being Australian is being a confident contributor to the global community, being resilient in the face of overwhelming odds and creating opportunities out of challenges and being competitive. Being Australian makes you part of one the most respected nations on the planet.

Being Australian means standing up for a fair go,

mateship, having a larrikin sense of humour, irreverence for authority, an adventurous spirit, a disdain for pretence and snobbery and a willingness to pitch in to help others less fortunate.
It means respecting the brave ANZACs who fought an unwinnable battle. As a nation and individuals we have a reputation as people who, when down, can pick ourselves back up and try again.

Now, more than in any time in our history, we punch above our weight on the global stage. We are respected as educated, honest, brave, hardworking people who have contributed great movies, written great books, painted great works of art and encouraged some of the greatest musicians and bands to perform.

Being Australian means being competitive but fair. We grow the best wool, beef, sugar, dairy and wine. We mine minerals that the world needs to support its population.

As Australians, we'll have a go at any sport, take on the whole world and often win. Our identity means beating the British at cricket and rugby league, New Zealand at rugby and netball the Americans at swimming and sailing and most importantly, we'll have a barbie at the end of it with our opponents.

All Australians can stand tall, mate, 'cos we are members of the one of the most respected people on earth. Being Australian is bloody awesome mate.

It received mix reviews. Some complained it was pithy others suggested it was a great start. It was my task to concentrate on the task and set the agenda ....kick the penalty.

It became obvious to me that numerical skills opened a new door with media and was a path to the voting public. I often asked evidence based questions developed from valid data sources. Such as "Why are federal seats restricted by state boundaries. Federal members don't answer to the state parliament or premier. Far from it – one plays for Australia and the other is playing Sheffield Shield." I also asked questions of voter equity and Our Fair Share of political representation.

Time for equal federal representation
Words: 378

VOTER equity is of increasing concern as our population grows and other jurisdictions' populations stagnate. Official population projections suggest that within 20 years Townsville's population will be larger than that of the whole Northern Territory.

The Northern Territory has two seats in federal Parliament – Lingiari and Solomon. The constitution apparently guarantees this.

At the 2013 election Lingiari elected a federal representative with less than 50,000 votes and Herbert elected a representative with more than 90,000. How can it be in a democratic society that one federal seat has 49,715 voters elect a representative and another 90,632? That's 40,917 more voters electing a representative in Herbert than in Lingiari. Yes Herbert has almost double the voters than Lingiari. That means our comparative voter right in Herbert is worth less than that of a Lingiari resident.

Kennedy is the largest electorate in Queensland and the second largest in the country. It spans from Townsville's northern beaches to south of Cairns and out to the Northern Territory border. It's so large the member needs to have two offices, one in Mt Isa and the other in Innisfail.

As population increases the maximum limit for our five North Queensland seats will be challenged. Lingiari isn't going to have this challenge any time soon.

But here's the issue, our federal seats are bounded by state borders. There is no good reason for this. The members don't answer to the state parliament or premier. Far from it – one plays for Australia and the other is playing Sheffield Shield.

So if we are playing for Australia why don't we forget the jurisdictional boundaries and allow federal electorates to represent similar groups of people?
Kennedy, for example, has urban coastal dwellers and dry country rural residents. Lingiari is mostly rural except for Alice Springs and Christmas Island. The rural portion of Kennedy should combine with Lingiari and form a new seat. I'm sure we could find 40,000 rural Kennedy voters out there.
Then we can adjust Leichardt, Herbert and Dawson and create a new seat in North Queensland. This new seat would cater for North Queensland population growth and provide a more equitable representation model for Australia. This would be a positive step in the direction of our fair share of federal parliament representation.

My statement "We vote for politicians to make our lives better. At the moment we treat our pets better than our terminally ill loved ones. If your pet has a terminal illness, a vet can assist with a dignified and painless exit." Is emotional rather than my usual evidence based style.

The weekly structure of his column was well considered. It revealed a diverse and organised narrative with the configuration as an economic frame, followed by population frame then an

emotional column that either raised or dropped the readers emotions.

This column followed an economic column, then a demographic one and demonstrated the complexity and depth of Our Fair share concept.

Pets get a better deal than patients
Words: 315

IF you are male and over 50, have you had a recent prostate exam?
More than three years ago my 85-year-old father died of prostate cancer. He was diagnosed as terminally ill in November 2010 and was expected to be dead by Christmas that year. He was a brave man who contributed to this country and deserved to die with dignity. Unfortunately this did not happen.
As the cancer aggressively destroyed his bladder, a well-intentioned doctor prolonged his life by attaching a catheter to a urethra tube. He lived the remainder of his eight weeks in an undignified state surrounded by the love of his family.
While I cherished every moment of time I had with my father, I couldn't help but think there was a better way for the terminally ill to die. We vote for politicians to make our lives better. At the moment we treat our pets better than our terminally ill loved

ones. If your pet has a terminal illness, a vet can assist with a dignified and painless exit.

Recently Senator Richard Di Natale tabled a new euthanasia bill, eighteen years after a law making euthanasia legal in the Northern Territory was overturned by federal Parliament, led by conservative Kevin Andrews.

This current draft bill relies on Section 51 of the Australian Constitution, which gives the Federal Parliament the power to legislate regarding medical services.

The bill sets up a "dying with dignity medical service" and authorises medical practitioners to prescribe, prepare and/or administer a substance that would assist a terminally ill person to end their life in a humane manner. While this may benefit some terminally ill people, we simultaneously need to protect our medical workers, doctors and nurses from prosecution.

As a nation and community, and as more people live into their eighties, we need to be brave and discuss euthanasia for terminally ill loved ones and ourselves.

In the above column I relate my experience of a dying family member with decisions politicians make. It raises an issue that can be solved by politicians, in Federal and State Parliaments. It's still a contentious issue. I had to oppose many people about how I would vote if elected to state parliament during the 2009 election. My response was I needed to see any legislation

before I could vote on it. Many people didn't like this, they had a closed mind.

The article below is an April Fools day joke column printed in 2014.

We've got Our Fair Share
Words: 421

LAST week I had a meeting with Premier and the Prime Minister.
They said they enjoyed reading my column and agreed that Brisbane and Canberra have been ripping the North off for the past 17 years. They indicated they would say sorry in both their parliaments.
I presented a paper that quantified our contribution to the state and national economy.
It indicated that we punch above our weight and that during the Beattie-Bligh rule over $1 billion was redistributed from the productive north to the less productive but populous south.
I then put forward the notion that the North should get our fair share. After all, we are arguably the second most productive region in the nation behind Western Australia.
Well, they looked at each other and talked to their advisers and finally we shook hands on a monumental agreement.

The North will get an audit of infrastructure, including an assessment of future needs. Those among us who believe in determining our own destiny can put our prosecution drinks down and celebrate because there's no more to fight about. They've agreed to back pay the North and future proof our fair share plus allow us a seat around the COAG table and one member on the RBA board. We are also getting a quarterly CPI index, because it's about time our cost of living was monitored, compared and market failures acted on by Brisbane and Canberra. Home insurance costs will be fixed.

The Queensland Government will help build a private sector baseload power station in the North creating more affordable power for new industry, creating thousands of new jobs and reducing the cost of living of northern households.

A stadium and iconic arts build that houses a casino, convention centre, gallery and accommodation will be fast tracked and built on the banks of the Ross Creek.

Redundant defence personnel located in the south will be transferred to Townsville, bolstering the largest army barracks in Australia. Federal and state public servants will be relocated out of Canberra and Brisbane and positioned closer to industry they serve.

They agreed to fund a Townsville-based social facility lobby group and to close the life expectancy gap between northern residents and their southern cousins, while encouraging better outcomes for the next generation with better education facilities and

opportunities. After all, a smarter healthy population is a more productive population and the more we contribute the better our fair share of the budget.
My job as an economist is done this April Fool's Day.
I can retire early.

I studied economics at James Cook University of North Queensland. In third year my regional economic lecturer Prof Harris introduced me to the constitution and some of the regional disparities it supported. My honors thesis title was regional disparities in Queensland local government areas.

Prof taught me, the person who asks the first question is the most important person along the road to change.

This next article demonstrated depth and horizontal complexity of the Our Fair Share concept by combining political, demographic and economic evidence to prosecute for better representation and constitutional reform.

Territory gerrymander unfair to us
Words: 406

LAST week I challenged the inequities in the Constitution with Tasmania receiving far more representation than North Queensland. To reinforce my point that the constitution needs reforming, Tasmania isn't the only jurisdiction with a gerrymander advantage.

The Northern Territory has enviable comparative federal political representation.

They and Tasmania are not the only examples of the current and future gerrymander supported by an outdated Constitution.

When we compare North Queensland to the Northern Territory we find similar gerrymander results to Tasmania; reinforcing my opinion that the Constitution needs reform to reflect contemporary Australian society.

In 2011, the Northern Territory had a population of 231,331 which was growing at around 1.5 per cent per annum. To put this in perspective, this population is roughly the same size as the Greater Townsville region, which in 2011 had a revised population of 225,137 with population growth outpacing the territories at 1.9 per cent.

If we extend the population boundaries to that area of Queensland north of the Tropic of Capricorn then the population dwarfs the Territory's, indeed it is almost four times larger than the Northern Territories population.

The Territory has an amazingly generous representative ratio. The Northern Territory has two Lower House seats and two senators with approximately 120,000 voters. That's a representation of around one is to 30,000 in federal parliament.

North Queensland has seven representatives with a representative ratio of one is to 72,000. It gets worse – their two Lower House seats are among the smallest in the 150-seat parliament and if you tally the numbers of people who voted in the 2013 election it's around the same as that for one seat in North Queensland. North Queensland seats rank in the top 30 per cent for voter enrolments and are growing faster than the national average.

If the Northern Territory wants to play the parochial card in the North Australia debate they need to check the facts before they open their mouths. We are all in this innovative opportunity together and no one should be sensitive about this information except maybe North Queenslanders.

Townsville is the largest city in North Australia and looks likely to continue that trend if we obtain our fair share of public and private investment, which can be improved by how many voices we have in parliament and how effective our representatives prosecute our case.

Darwin might be the capital of the Territory but Townsville is the capital of North Australia.

Regions like Townsville have experienced long delays in gaining facilities and services that southern cities take for granted. In this column I elaborate on the political barriers to economic commonsense. My experience as a respected economist and political leader with familiarity in dealing with layers of political decisions permits me to write this column. There can't be

that many Regional Economists with strong political experience. It also highlights the comparison between economics and political decisions.

Because Queensland is decentralised regional city's may never obtain similar facilities to large cities, however, politicians have the power to override economics.

Bypass Brisbane for our own good

Words: 435

WE need to keep past, present and future Brisbane honest about our fair share of any proceeds from possible lease of public assets. As I analyse the language being used, if the Townsville community rejects the sale of the port by voting out some or all of the LNP representatives but the LNP resumes power (or Labor wins) in Brisbane at the next state election then there is a solid chance we could lose the lot.

There is already a strong wedge being developed by Brisbane on the lease proceeds. Conservative Brisbane could use a state wide re-election win as a mandate to sell our port but with the possibility after the next state election of three non-LNP members, they could give nothing to Townsville. Yes prepare for a protracted almighty wedge.

Why would conservative Brisbane give a massive economic boost to our region and make non-LNP members look good – politically stupid. And why would conservative Cant-berra provide funds to make non-LNP members and councillors look good? They would frame the fiscal argument such that it would be non-LNP members' and councillors' fault and wedge the community for political change. Unfortunately this means long delays to boost our economy.

This scenario has a precedent. A similar situation occurred back in the 1980s when Premier Joh promised Townsville over $200 million to build a resort on Florence Bay. The community rejected the proposal and voted out Tourism Minister Max Hooper as member for Townsville. Joh was voted back in Brisbane. A bit miffed about losing Tourism Minister Max, he promptly diverted funds to other centres and also the location of the North Queensland international airport.

There are many other examples of this regional public investment political wedging such as the PET scanner, Blakeys crossing and Jezzine Barracks funding. Some of these examples took years for the different politics at different levels of government to align before the project could advance for the benefit of the people. The sooner we find a way to bypass Brisbane the better off voters in our region and the rest of North Queensland are going to be.

We need to keep past, present and future Brisbane honest about our fair share of any proceeds from possible lease of these assets. The more I hear present Brisbane say the money is going into a regional development fund with different pots of money the more I think our money could end up developing other regions, maybe even the Gold Coast. The Gold Coast or Cairns could laugh all the way to prosperity funded by Townsville with the decision made 1500km away in Brisbane.

During the time I wrote the Our Fair Share column I was occasionally contacted by different leaders with important information. In this column a local councilor covertly supplies information to assist in asking questions about APS staff attrition.

North deserves more from its pollies

Words: 412

DON'T let the economic headlights knock you down like a startled cane toad; times are tough in Australia's largest northern city and they are going to get tougher, at least in the short term.

When I polish up my Australian-made economic crystal ball and look at the Townsville jobs market, the challenges outweigh the opportunities. The highest unemployment rate in Queensland, with a three-month average of 10 per cent, youth unemployment over 20 per cent, indigenous unemployment over 15 per cent, over-50s unemployment climbing and under-employment endemic.

Over the coming months, the events season will stall, school leavers will start looking for work, the wet season will slow what local construction activity there is, hinder mining and transport and reduce tourism and associated activity. Then there's the state election effect that will dampen both business and consumer confidence.

Recently, coal mines in the Galilee Basin shed around 1000 jobs due mainly to a world glut of coal, and last Wednesday the Australian Public Service revealed an annualised cut of 8000 jobs; around half were from natural attrition.

So I asked our four local federal representatives about the gross and net APS job change in Townsville over the past 12 months. Mr Christensen and Mr Katter's offices responded they would follow up.

Nationally, the Government expects the public service will reduce by 16,500 staff before July 2017. It means another 8575 public service jobs will go nationally over the next three years.

I also asked two supplementary questions.

Can you tell me how many of these future APS job losses are earmarked for Townsville?

Can you let me know what you are doing to stimulate the Townsville economy and create sustainable jobs in Townsville in the next 12 months?

As thousands of new job seekers enter the market and become eligible to vote, we hear that our economic compass should point more to China than Cant-berra. While I agree China should be on our economic radar, pointing our compass to China is simplistic and fraught with many challenges.

Cant-berra has a problem with the message its sending North Queenslanders. When you work hard and contribute we are one, but when your economic resilience is tested, look to others for salvation.

Cant-berra needs to quantify the contribution North Queensland makes to the Federal Budget and then recognise our fair share of fiscal allocations. It also needs to provide a cost-of-living index for Townsville, and a regional Australian representative on the monetary policy-important RBA board.

A new state, consistent with section 124 of the constitution was a fundamental frame of my writing, research and columns. My thesis supervisor Professor Harris and colleague Dr Peter Crossman encouraged strong evidence based research and policy development. I use this skill and a different approach to create discussion on new states in Australia. A separate Scotland was in the news because it was holding a referendum for independence. In this essay I was using current international news to challenge the way we think about Australia.

Scotland a shining beacon of hope

Words: 338

THE people of Scotland will vote in a referendum on Thursday.

They will be asked the “Yes/No” question: “Should Scotland be an independent country?” What a brilliant example of positive democratic process. The world owes Scotland a vote of thanks.

For six months it has staged a festival of democracy and an Edinburgh tattoo of argument. It has demonstrated that democratic participation is important and the passion to progress peacefully dominates.

Scotland is not alone in its quest for independence; there are places all over the world seeking autonomy. They are looking to Scotland’s democratic style for inspiration.

This is probably why Australia’s Prime Minister thought it was appropriate to enter the debate.

The Canadian prime minister has also entered the debate, because they have a continuing opportunity with Quebec.

The enthusiasm for self-government remains strong in Quebec and the most recent vote for independence in the 1990s was lost by less than 1 per cent.

Other examples of democratic provincial struggle include, Catalan in Spain which has been arguing with Madrid for more self-rule for decades, Bavaria in Germany has aspirations, North California and part of Oklahoma are discussing how they can obtain statehood.

Italy it seems is a hotchpotch of different linguistic regions and cultures that is ready to challenge the status quo.
There are many examples of successful jurisdictional divorce such as Ireland, East Timor, Bougainville and Telangana in India, but unfortunately most of these new jurisdictions chose a different path to the peaceful one Scotland advocates.
The most recent Scottish polls indicate a closer outcome than previously thought and it seems momentum is with the Yes vote.
If I had a vote I would vote yes because of the economic and political long-term net benefits for Scotland.
I would vote yes because I believe in democracy and regional autonomy.
Scotland is defining a unique style of contemporary democracy.

Whatever deal follows the vote this Thursday, there will still be a Scotland but a Scotland that commands respect on the world stage of democratic confrontation.

Daylight saving is a contentious issue in South East Queensland. Southern Queensland seem to desire it, but regional Queensland doesn't. A state plebiscite on the issue failed in 1988/89. It failed on geographic boundaries. In this essay, I raise the issue that if the south wants Daylight saving does it want two daylight time periods in

the one state or two new states?

Daylight saving not yet put to rest

Words: 365

THERE have been multiple attempts to bring daylight saving to Queensland after its adoption was voted down at the 1992 state referendum, which recorded a 54.5 per cent "no" vote. Yet our distant southern cousins remain restless, and you could be mistaken for thinking that they want to break away from the north.

Daylight saving is a contemporary Queensland issue, and if a state referendum on daylight saving for south Queensland was held today I have no doubt that with the population changes that have occurred over the past 22 years, it would be passed this time on the strength of increased numbers in the south.

Population in the south has increased by around 1.3 million to about 3.7 million and increased by 280,000 north of the Fiztroy to about a million. There might be a small adjustment for western Queensland, but essentially the strength of numbers in the south would pass a daylight saving referendum if it were held today.

Still, most of north and western Queensland don't want and don't need daylight saving.

Well I'm a supporter of daylight saving for south Queensland, but I'm not an advocate for daylight saving in North Queensland.

I experienced daylight saving in 1989 in Townsville and frankly it didn't make that much difference to my life. However, the daylight savings trial revealed that some industries suffered, such as restaurants. Curiously, because of the extra hour of sunlight, we northerners reduced the amount of times we went out to dinner. It had something to do with people's eating habits and not wanting to eat until the sun went down.

So as we still got hungry at the same time, we ate a meal at home rather than going out to eat while the sun was up.

But I can see Brisbane's dilemma, It needs to compete with Sydney and Melbourne, so there would be an economic and social benefit for the south with similar business hours.

But North Queensland doesn't need it, and there may be social and economic costs for our community.

Bring on a referendum, I say, and let the Queensland people decide if south Queensland should get daylight saving in line with southern states.

The next essay raises the challenges of a large modern decentralized state. Half the population live outside Brisbane and almost 1 million live in the five statistical divisions north of Gladstone. In this column, I ask the reader a leading Our Fair Share question.....but as parts of the North are continually being undervalued, there is growing sentiment and evidence that, in

the future, the North should challenge the Constitution in order to obtain a suitable outcome. Which poses a further puzzle, what is a suitable outcome?

Progress depends on the Constitution
Words: 341

CONSTITUTIONAL reform needs to be high on the agenda of this week's North Australia forum. Many, if not all, of the speakers come from the far south and wouldn't know what it's like to live here. Let's hope we reduce the academic aloofness and concentrate on real, sustainable and achievable progress.
The region north of the Fitzroy River is a prosperous, growing region that deserves better recognition for its economic, environmental and social contribution. It may be difficult to separate a historical link that has existed since before federation, but as parts of the North are continually being undervalued, there is growing sentiment and evidence that in the future the North should challenge the Constitution in order to obtain a suitable outcome. Which poses a further puzzle, what is a suitable outcome?
• Abolish the second tier of government and adopt a regional council of mayors?
• Establish a new state?
• Re-establish the state Upper House that in part represents regional and North Queensland?

• Reform the Constitution so there's one senator for every two Lower House seats?
• Add another Lower House seat in North Queensland and increase the senatorial representation?
The current state and federal fiscal allocation system provides poor outcomes for regions far from Brisbane and Canberra. It follows that for social and economic progress to occur, North Queensland needs a better system of representation and fairer share of public expenditure than it is currently receiving.
Those among us who argue that "if it's not broken there's no need to fix it" should look at:
• Lower average life spans for Northerners.
• Consistently poorer education performances.
• Road and rail challenges.
• Inability to obtain necessary economic development infrastructure funding.
We need a brave leader to continue the robust debate on constitutional reform at this northern development conference.
That person and our community must never give up and they must recognise that the journey will be long and challenging but in the end the North needs its fair share of representation within a flexible constitutional framework.

In my final column I prosecute for Our Fair Share of political representation in my new definition of North Queensland, in particular the senate. I reinforce the concept of constitutional

reform to influence the reader to think about how the constitution could change our lives for the better. I point to section 7 of the constitution and reveal that after the next federal election there will only be 1 senator north of Rockhampton. LNP and ALP react to this evidence. LNP place a senator in Rockhampton and the ALP transfer someone from Brisbane to Cairns. I feel that my advocacy made a difference and influenced decision makers that improved regional representation.

Stating case for our own chamber
Words: 412

I HAVE researched North Queensland's economy for more than 30 years defining its boundaries, quantifying and communicating its economic contribution and feeling its strengths and weaknesses. I have concluded that the North needs a new path with a new force.
After carefully comparing North Queensland's situation to other jurisdictions and punctiliously considering the benefits and costs of various solutions to our northern challenges, I find the best solution is to bring decision-making governance with economic foundation to the people. That is, supported by section 121 to 124 of the Constitution, forming a new state.

Part of this solution requires the creation of a fresh new North Queensland political force that represents Northerners first without the influence of Fitzbrisos.

Our political challenges are enormous but we need to change them to achieve our fair share of public finances. We can't rely on the tired old current combinations to change things. They keep doing the same things over and over with the same results.

Interestingly, Section 7 of the Constitution includes this important statement: "The Parliament of the State of Queensland, if that State be an Original State, may make laws dividing the State into divisions and determining the number of senators to be chosen for each division."

Have Brisdrain ever considered this? After the next Federal election there will be one fulltime Queensland senator north of Sarina; that is, one fulltime senator representing 700,000 Queenslanders. The average senatorial representation in Queensland, south of Sarina, is one to 365,000. North Queensland is so large with so many different regions, so many families, with so many different challenges how does one fulltime senator represent all this the same as a Brisdrain-based senator? It appears to be political disrespect.

Tasmania has 12 senators for 514,800 people, or one for just 42,900 people. And for fewer than 100,00 votes, the Northern Territory gets four representatives. It follows that for better social and economic progress to occur, North Queensland needs a better system of representation and a better share of public finances. As a separate jurisdiction, GST revenue would bypass Brisdrain and flow directly to the North. Mining royalties and other State public revenues would stay where they are produced.

One potential cost of a new state is that it may require more “bloody politicians”. But overwhelmingly this comparatively small cost would be enormously outweighed by the benefits accruing to the New State.

This is my final column, so Ooroo and may the new force be with you.

Many people contacted me to continue writing the Our Fair Share column. It was funny, clever and contained important information, they said. However, I could not provide the information without better compensation, and that wasn’t available, so the information became occasional but focused on current political, demographic and economic events.

At least one future editor would offer me an incentive to continue writing the Our Fair Share column. The offer included a column in all regional papers across my definition of North Queensland. I considered the opportunity but eventually declined the offer.

The following column identifies the benefits of political power combined with strong economic evidence. South Australia, a mendicant State, gets awarded most of a multi billion defence contract for our national submarine program. I use one of my favorite scenes in a movie to portray frustration at a comparatively productive region not receiving Our Fair Share.

We'll have what SA is having, thanks

Words: 444

WELCOME to my penultimate column and thank you for taking the time to read Our Fair Share.

Have you seen the movie *When Harry Met Sally?* My favourite scene is when Meg Ryan is faking the big "O" in a coffee shop and the neighbouring woman says "I'll have what she is having". Economics can be just as sexy and we all want our fair share. South Australia recently got Big O-type economic news that made me think we want what SA is having.

According to Queensland Treasury and DS Economics, there are more than 930,000 people living in North Queensland. Its economy contributes about $80 billion or 27 per cent of the State's economy. Each person living in the North contributes about $85,500, 50 per cent more than southern Queenslanders and about 30 per cent more than the rest of Australia.

Yet our unemployment rate is worse than the nation's, worse than Brisdrain's and interestingly worse than South Australia's, and yet South Australia gets a $40 billion economic orgasm with a navy ship building program. Economics can be Dead Sexy (DS)!

Recent ABS data reveals north of the Tropic of Capricorn there are 42,000 people unemployed, the unemployment rate is 9.3 per cent and if this region were a separate jurisdiction it would have the worst unemployment rate in Australia. So do we need economic viagra?

Currently South Australia has the worst state unemployment rate at 7.9 per cent. We are told that car industry downsizing will create more unemployment and, as a result, from 2020 a $40 billion navy ship building program will create thousands of jobs in South Australia. Economic viagra or political satisfaction?

With more people and being a state, South Australia is allocated more representation in parliament. They have 11 members and 12 senators to prosecute their case in Cantberra. They have obviously caught the ear of someone with more conversations than us because they aren't more attractive.

Next year North Queensland will lose one senator and reduce to one-third of South Australia's representation. So with more than half their population we get a third their representation in Cantberra.

Based on South Australia needing economic viagra, North Queensland needs several doses and better political representation. North Queensland has a greater unemployment rate and a significant downturn in several key regional industries. The North has been and will remain a faithful partner but we deserve better economic and political respect.

North Queensland is younger, more productive, more resilient and far better looking than South Australia; we don't want extra special treatment.

But like the line out of *When Harry Met Sally* – we'll have what South Australia is having, thanks.

Once again, I point out the obviousness in Townsville's branding absurdity in this column. Brilliant, experienced and educated professionals mucking up a simple brand. I also talk about open evidence based discussion on new states in Australia.

North can state its case at talkfest

Words: 438

IMAGINE all the university degrees and politician hours that have achieved the following brilliant outcome. We now have three levels of government with different definitions of North Queensland.

The Federal Government's white paper defines North Queensland as Queensland north of the Tropic of Capricorn. The Queensland Government defines North Queensland as the combination of local governments from Mackay northwards and locally we have Townsville Enterprise, largely supported by our local councils, promoting North Queensland as the five local councils in the ABS defined Townsville Region.

Yes all three levels of government agree to disagree on a simple and effective definition of North Queensland. If it weren't a serious marketing challenge for the Magnetic Coast it would be fodder for a comedy like *Yes Minister*.

Maybe the North Australia convention being held in Townsville can sort it out and maybe they can answer the question why there are no states in their definition of North Australia. States and capitals get all the GST and have major fiscal influence. Why not a state in North Australia that supports our people?

There needs to be open, educated and mature discussion about creating new states right across Australia to bring government closer to the people. Interestingly Queensland Senator Matt Canavan has joined the growing group of federal politicians who are prosecuting for more states in Australia.

Unsurprisingly this group comprises regional-based politicians supporting better government for all Australians.

When developed, the Constitution accommodated the creation of new states. The intention and vision was clear. There have been several attempts using sections of the Constitution to create new states and even for states to secede from the Commonwealth.

Each secessionist referendum has been worthwhile, because you don't get marked down for standing up for your region but more importantly some referendums and debates achieved significant fiscal rewards.

In 1933 Western Australia successfully voted for secession from Australia. They sent the bill off to London who promptly sent it back and asked 'Cantberra' to deal with it. 'Cantberra' rejected it but the reward for isolated prosperous Western Australia was the creation of the Commonwealth Grants Commission. We have those brave people to thank for enduring and improved state fiscal equalisation.

Is it time regional Australia prosecuted a similar case?

Apparently Senator Canavan plans to put a submission into the Federation White Paper, renewing the push for a new state "to better represent" Queensland's north.

This is a way to represent the people living in our region. There's a chance the separate state concept will succeed but what concession would you seek in return for loyalty? Access to direct GST distributions from the Federal Government?

In this essay, I use humour to belittle arrogant decision makers from Brisbane, renaming their city, Brisdrain. This is the first time the term Brisdrain is used (2013); It's sledging and I feel it had an influence. I don't take political sides just a philosophical view that we in the north haven't been getting Our Fair Share.

New seat needed to ensure fairness

Words: 372

YOU probably realise by now that I am sceptical that Brisdrain has our best interests at heart. There's a state political boundary redistribution looming and I'm sure you have an opinion. Your opinion is important. Why would we let someone over 1300 kilometres away determine our destiny? Given some basic facts I believe Magnetic Coast region deserves a new seat in state Parliament to catch up with predicted voter enrolment growth.

There are 89 seats in the State Parliament with no upper house to check that the regions aren't being short-changed by Brisdrain. Thirteen state seats (15 per cent) are located in North Queensland; five of those are in or around the Magnetic Coast region.

Our average voter enrolment is likely to be over the threshold in four of our five state seats and overall our region is likely to be almost 5 per cent above the mean threshold limit. There are over 157,000 state voters in Magnetic Coast region. The expected average number of voters for each electorate in March next year is 31,445; the threshold is 30,000. Given these facts, I believe, the best option for our region is to create a new seat in the fast-growing northern beaches location, boost our representation in State Parliament and reduce the strength of the far southeast.

If there was an additional seat it would reduce the northern voter average per seat to about 26,200, similar to southern seats such as Mansfield, Woodridge and Indooroopilly. Importantly, it could provide a better result for Northerns especially since we lack an upper house or regional checking house. Queensland hasn't had a state political boundary redistribution for around seven years and it's time we got an extra seat. While we are creating a new northern seat we could redistribute voters in the southeast to abolish a SEQ seat. The new state seat on the Magnetic Coast could be called Richards after Tom Richards, a local World War I hero, gold medal-winning Olympian and Wallaby.

The state electoral redistribution will commence in February 2016, there will be opportunities for all North Queenslanders to make suggestions and I'm sure there will be a variety of opinions on how to prosecute for our fair share and keep Brisdrain honest.

Once again I discuss branding and the mix messages investors and tourists get when southern media discuss North Queensland.

Time to move away from NQ brand

Words: 396

AS you enter the largest city in North Australia a big blue sign greets drivers with “welcome to Townsville Capital of North Queensland”.

At last count there are three definitions of North Queensland.

The NQ brand for our region is confusing for locals, investors, media and travellers and it needs to change.

Consistency is imperative when branding a city or product.

The brand North Queensland as a headline title for our region doesn’t provide a competitive advantage in promotional opportunities.

So where the bloody hell is North Queensland? The longest standing definition of North Queensland is Queensland north of the 22nd parallel.

This is the first definition of North Queensland and it goes back to the booming 1890s when a bill was passed by the legislative assembly in Brisbane to create three new states; South Queensland, Central Queensland and North Queensland.

The bill was sent to the colonial office in London but returned.

After that came the definition of North Queensland which includes Burdekin, Charters Towers Hinchinbrook, Palm Island and Townsville. This area aligns with the ABS or officially used

Australian Standard Geographical Classification of Northern Queensland now called Townsville Region.
Then in 2008 I wrote an essay, Existential North Queensland. In that paper I defined North Queensland as the statistical divisions north of Fitzroy and out to the NT border.
Some politicians and organisations have adopted this definition. This makes three definitions of North Queensland.
My point is there are so many definitions of North Queensland that the brand is too confusing.
When southern media do a story up here they use North Queensland for Cairns, Mackay, Townsville out to Mount Isa.
This makes it difficult to brand our city and region with the term North Queensland without confusing most Australians.
We can't fight this or re-educate the south. The branding issue has been continuing for too long and a simple realignment could boost our marketing advantage.
North Queensland should remain where it was originally intended to be, that portion of Queensland north of the 22nd parallel.
The official Northern region has been renamed the Townsville region and we should get on board.
That area north of Fiztroy could be called Capricornia or the Great Eastern Frontier (Thanks Mr Hockey). Townsville needs to align our region with a stronger, more representative and sexy

brand like the Australian Mediterranean, Sunshine City, Adventure Capital or, simply, Tropadise.

Its been said to me that I was a shrewd political influencer with a north Queensland compass. I wasn't rusted on to any political party but could navigate their economic and social policies with easy reference to Townsville and regional Queensland. There's a great political joke in this article. I also ridicule Canberra as Cantberra for the first time in 2014.

Blueberries at risk of being off-colour
Words: 358

IT'S funny, when you reveal a defect in your physical makeup, such as colour blindness, some people connect with you and others take advantage of an imperfection.

Some like to sledge and, you know what, it's all character building.

One of my tennis buddies, who will remain nameless, suggested that my line calls should be automatically overruled because of my colour recognition imperfection. I reject this form of sledging and substitute my own. I've been taught which colour is what and I identify the same colours as everyone else. It's probably just a different version of what the colour-perfect see.

Anyway, our iridescent paradise needs some attention from the upcoming federal Budget and the colour scheme is on red or blue alert, depending on your degree of colour appreciation limitation.

Thanks to everyone who sent in ideas for the community facility needs register. I have collected more than 30 different ideas, including better incentives for CBD developers, a performing arts and movie-making complex, using the existing heavy-gauge rail network for public transport, a North Queensland home insurance entity (go Warren Entsch who secured $500k for a feasibility study), solar panels on every Townsville roof, lights on the new Nelly Bay walking track, better aged care facilities – and the list continues.

There's six weeks to go until the Budget. If we haven't submitted a list of projects or discussed Townsville's community facility needs with "Cantberra" by now, we probably have little chance of getting much from this far-off frozen land. Still, it's worth mentioning that our piece of paradise is the intersection for three federal seats and one senator. They are mostly Blueberries (LNP).

If the Blueberries want to keep their representation in Parliament they need to demonstrate how they will develop paradise. With all the commotion going on in Cantberra at present, I would not rule out an early election and if the correct political frame is in place after this Budget, a double dissolution isn't unthinkable.

As the Governor of the Reserve Bank said recently, monetary policy is becoming ineffective and the economy needs a complementary fiscal boost.

I wonder if this bloke is colourblind too?

In this article I talk about a Social Facilities group and use the story of a shipwrecked sailor who is washed up on Cape Cleveland and rescued by Aborigines. Jemmy Morrell lived with them for over a decade, experiencing crocodile attacks, poor transport and bad health conditions. My combined political and economic experience allows me to see that social facilities are out of political decision maker mind until an election comes around and I raise challenges and a solution to this problem.

United we can make a real difference

Words: 461

A UNITED community is much stronger than a divided one. Together we can make a difference for current residents and future generations, but divided we fail ourselves and our children. I received many responses last week regarding infrastructure and service concepts for Townsville and our region; a cohesive community has the power to achieve them more efficiently.

One suggestion was we establish a film complex as part of a greater arts precinct that has a unique building and distinctive purpose. This suggestion included a film about James Morrell, an 1800s shipwrecked Englishman who lived with Aborigines

around Townsville and Bowen. A group has written to Russell Crowe suggesting this. *Townsville Bulletin's* Steve Price has also penned for such a project.
This is a positive and passionate effort by a few to improve Townsville's international and national reputation, create sustainable jobs and improve our lifestyle. If it works it would boost confidence much more than a short visit from a foreign prince. While a small group can make a difference a larger united organisation would solidify any potential net benefits.
While many suggestions were for buildings or capital expenditure, many were also social and lifestyle-enhancing. We have several organisations that work for economic development and public investment but we don't have an entity that focuses on social facilities and opportunities like the arts, international students, sporting capacities, public hospital facilities or education standards. Complementing the film complex suggestion I would like to suggest a social facilities lobby group that would unite the many hardworking Townsville community organisations and create something unique in Australia. It would be an independent organisation that unites a large part of our community; a stronger voice for social facilities and services in Townsville.
The Townsville Social Facility Organisation would inform everyone about the well-researched needs in their location, their costs and benefits, the

maintenance requirements on facilities and facilities required to support current and future populations.
So instead of begging for an economically unconvincing Coliseum, or whetting our lips over a foreign prince we would have a group that focuses on better public transport, lower home insurance premiums, improved health outcomes and a more united, healthy, educated, sustainable, happy and independent community.
A proper facility and service delivery audit for Townsville would reduce the impact of public investment thought bubbles that are driven by three-year political cycles. Rather than waiting for an election to frame an argument for scarce private and public funds and wedge the community into a "do this or don't get that facility", we need to be proactive and unite the Townsville community to achieve sustainable jobs, improve everyone's lifestyle and achieve better health, education and economic outcomes. Together Townsville can do amazing things; divided we fail ourselves and future generations.
Happy St Patrick's Day.

Another cracker of a political column. What's a Fitzbriso? "A Fitzbriso is someone who has a foot in Townsville, a foot in Brisbane and their precious family fruit dangle in the Fitzroy River."

NQ politics is like a bowl of fruit salad
Words: 426

WE have just finished a short democratic festival and it's time for the north to harvest its fiscal fruit.
We all know it's a very serious matter obtaining Our Fair Share but to help you smile I have gathered a few friendly political jibes.
As someone from Cantberra with above average intelligence once said "life is like a box of chocolates" but in North Queensland, politics is like a bowl of fruit.
Fellow mangos, blueberries, strawberries, bananas, apples and watermelons, let's share a smile.
The Tories have a hilarious name for the Greens
They've nicknamed them Watermelons. Watermelons are green on the outside and red on the inside. Politics can be hard for the communally sensitive, but a clever jibe can be a friendly way to get your message across.
I wonder what fruit you could call a Tory? What about blueberries? Plump fruit on the outer branches with their roots anchored a long distance away.
The Labor Party could be immature strawberries? They might be red on the outside but their inner flesh is not yet ready?
PUP has to be a banana, with some nutritious policies but you can slip up on the discarded peel.
And KAP. What about a red apple? One where the northern half is juicier than the southern half.
Still "watermelons" may be the best political sledge I've heard recently.

North Queensland politics can be just as much fun. Framing and wedging are far more sophisticated and parochial than southern politics.
In general northerners are a parochial bunch of mangos and we prefer the Bowen variety to the southern common. Overall we don't like "sort of northern" politicians because of their blurred commitment. I have a sledge for these "sort of" or hollow representatives, FiztBrisos and Cantberrans. A Fitzbriso is someone who has a foot in Townsville, a foot in Brisbane and their precious family fruit dangle in the Fitzroy River. A Cantberran is someone who constantly knocks back feasible infrastructure or subsidies for the north that exist down south with the term "We can't do that ..."
Now if we ever get a mango politician that understands and delivers our fair share both long run and short term then we'd have a berry special person. We would reserve a special place in our fruitful hearts for that effective person who can deliver what northerners need rather than delivering what Brisdrain or Cantberra tell us we can't have.
Fellow mangos, blueberries, strawberries, bananas, apples and watermelons, share a smile and enjoy all the different varieties of fruit our paradise produces.

This next essay is a clever political saga of an unexpected political win by a bumbling opposition leader..... the seemingly bumbling leader of the Strawberry gang doesn't quite

know what she's got herself into. She's done a Bradbury and her smile tells it all. If you dont know what a Bradbury is, Google it. Many elections are lost by incumbentes, rather than won by better candidates with better policy.

It'll end in tears, bed-hopping pollies
Words: 372

HAVE you seen the movie *Pulp Fiction*? It's a combination of bizarre simultaneous events, unusually connected, that culminate in tragedy.
Welcome to the political version of this contemporary opera unfolding in Australia.
There's always a love story in *Pulp Fiction*. Eleven days ago, Queenslanders fell out of love with the LNP. While 51 per cent of the primary vote was cast for the Blueberries, they are back in the dating market with a familiar leader.
Meanwhile, the seemingly bumbling leader of the Strawberry gang doesn't quite know what she's got herself into with her new relationship. She's done a Bradbury and her smile tells it all.
Blueberry family members panicked. Territorian cousins, spooked by the dumping, tried unsuccessfully to topple the head of their family. Canberran family members were so surprised by the Queensland break-up they took sides in their relationship crisis. Maybe they could use their own $200 family relationship voucher to obtain counselling?

Consistent with *Pulp Fiction* standards, there's always several alternative partners competing for the attention of a central character. In this version, the main alternative lover is conspicuous by their absence. They are definitely seeking the favours of the entity that dropped the arrogant companion. The curiously similar thing about politics and relationships is the more things change, the more they stay the same; I'm betting the federal alternative won't do a Bradbury next year.

Pulp fiction loves unusual twists and in the northeastern province, Mr Springborg has re-emerged as the new leader of the Blueberries.

Concurrently and curiously, KAP came out last week and said it wanted to redirect funding from a siblings-proposed stadium to a northwestern Queensland project. There is also farce in *Pulp Fiction*, and as Homer Simpson puts it, DOH! This potential alternative should look down south instead of stealing from their own household.

So as this story of political pulp fiction concludes, we seek the tragic ending. We find it in such a small margin to govern the northeastern province. One by-election, one Thompsongate, one Nuttallgate or something else incredibly pulp fictionist, such as the Mary Rose affair, and we are all back looking for a new relationship earlier than expected. Sometimes we get more than our fair share of political pulp fiction.

In this essay, I discuss a facility that politicians withhold due to some form of political

difference and how these decision makers hold our city and other regions to political ransom or blackmail. They've done it for decades and no one has questioned the logic in how Townsville or any regional centre gets adequate fiscal attention.... Referring to the proposed Stadium, "*There is political strategy in this economically unconvincing proposal. The new state government will probably ask their federal political opponents to contribute the other money and wedge the community before the next federal election, due next year.*

I dislike political ransoms. It diminishes positive economic progress.

I correctly predict that the next federal election in Townsville (2016), will be about a new stadium. Few people are aware of the role I played in gaining funding for the stadium. Initially I was against the stadium saying spend it on something that will benefit more people. If we combined several ineffective projects like The Cruiseship Terminal ($87m), The Stadium ($293m), Ried Park car racing track ($35m), Townsville CBD Mall ($57m) and Jezzine Barracks ($40m) the city would have over half a billion dollars to invest in a really significant job supporting economic diversifying project.

I sought coalitions of media to prosecute worthwhile causes and keep the bastards honest.

We got it right, let's hope MPs do too
Words: 430

AS a local politician once said "The voters always get it right". There were many factors that contributed to an amazing state LNP loss.

Most Northerners wanted jobs but didn't want public assets leased; but most of all, we didn't like being held to political ransom in exchange for less than Our Fair Share.

The northern message was clear – Bugger off Brisdrain.

We northerners are fed up with unacceptably high unemployment and low consumer confidence linked to insecure jobs. We are outraged that more than a fair share of public funds continues to be spent down south. Most of the community have voted for a different direction.

Democracy is the real winner although the northern economy may not be.

Last week I made some predictions. I got some right and some wrong. I was wrong predicting Mr Crisafulli and Mr Cox could be promoted but I was right predicting that a seemingly arrogant Campbell Newman would no longer be premier. Paradoxically, I hope I am right that having three government members in Townsville will benefit us economically.

With the LNP loss, Townsville receives $100 million for a slowly built, economically unconvincing, stadium over the next three years.
Unfortunately, $100 million is less than half of what is needed to build a new stadium and seemingly keep the NQ Cowboys in Townsville.
There is political strategy in this economically baffling proposal. The new state government will probably ask their federal political opponents to contribute the other $110 million and wedge the community before the next federal election, due next year.
I dislike political ransoms. It diminishes positive economic progress that benefits real people and regional communities. They hold Townsville to ransom yet again.
So is the stadium in jeopardy? I have been told by a reliable source that the federal government doesn't do stadiums. Indeed the most any federal government has committed to a stadium is around $25 million.
Even if we CPI that figure we don't get $110 million. Unfortunately, I expect more political ransom on this facility.
So while Northern voters got it right last Saturday, let's hope southern politicians heard the message about political ransoms.
Finally, while Townsville might now be home to the new Assistant Minister for North Queensland, Cairns may get the State Treasurer. I know which one I would rather have, but let's not prejudge the new state cabinet or next state budget just yet.

Congratulations to incoming state members, I hope you achieve Our Fair Share of public funding, represent Townsville region in Brisdrain and are not just your party's messenger in Paradise.

In this next essay I use my years of political experience to forecast the 2015 state election and I get some right and some wrong.

The voters never get it wrong

Words: 336

ECONOMISTS try hard not to get involved in politics but alas the politicians have grabbed the dismal science and thrust it onto the front pages of our tabloids.

To be honest economists were only created so weather forecasters would look good.

So with diminished marginal perception, I dabble in politics.

With four days to go until our version of the contemporary democratic festival I have a forecast about which party will win the state election. But more interesting than which party will win, is who will be Premier.

I don't believe Campbell Newman will be Premier after Saturday but I also don't believe Annastacia Palaszczuk will be. On Sunday 1st February I think the premiership of Queensland will be a competition between Laurence Springborg and Tim Nicholls and I think the Borg will have the numbers. Another interesting forecast relating to Saturday's election will be a changing of the ministerial guards. There is likely to be a cabinet reshuffle after this election and in this humble economist's crystal ball gazing forecast Mr Crisafulli could be in line for a promotion to possibly Treasurer or Health while the well-performing Mr Cox is a possible chance of picking up Minister for Agriculture. Political forecasts aside, the worst possible economic outcome for Townsville this state election is not a hung parliament – it is having three MPs who are not members of the victorious party in Brisdrain.

If this occurs, the stadium will be postponed until another election; poor consumer and business confidence will endure; job insecurity will stagnate and unacceptably high unemployment will continue as population growth stumbles.

Ultimately, the driver we need to boost our confidence will be postponed. Having three non-government MPs will be as useful as sleeves on a singlet.

Remember after Saturday's democratic festival there will still be a Queensland; the Premier will be a politician and it will rain last Thursday. With hindsight only 10 per cent of economists get it right. It's just never the same 10% of economists. Smile. It's Tuesday.

In true Diogenes fashion (cynic) I point out the reality of decision making after

elections.......*the worst possible outcome for Townsville after an election is to have MPs who are not members of the victorious party.* Voters generally select parties and their leaders. In Australia we have pseudo presidential elections. In some election its preferences that decide who will be PM or Premier. Its important for a core number of voters to sit on the fence. This means those seats become marginal and are 'in play', politically. They are decided by preferences and that means the political bargaining for economic development can start. An example might help. The current member for Hinchinbrook came fourth in the primary vote, yes fourth, in that seat in 2017 state election. The candidate who came fifth did a preference deal with him and because he polled ahead of the fifth place person, he collected his preferences. This allowed fourth to leapfrog third and collect their preferences and then second and collect their preferences and eventually win the seat of Hinchinbrook. If you're considering running at an election Its important to do your preference strategy and deals early.

Whoever wins, they must fight for us

Words: 472

WILL they just be their party's messenger in Townsville?

Do you remember when Mal Meninga stood as a political candidate in the ACT? He reconsidered mid campaign and said: “I’m buggered, I’m sorry.” It may have been the shortest political career in history.

Even so, I thought Big Mal was precisely the sort of person we need in Parliament: a solid communicator and a strong strategist, someone with positive values who could represent his electorate in Parliament. This election is about many issues but the most important one, in my opinion, is will your candidate represent us in Brisdrain, or will they just be their party’s messenger in Townsville, the largest city in North Australia?

All our local candidates need to be congratulated for having the courage and passion to want to represent our region in Brisdrain. They are trying to make a difference and they deserve our respect.

Last week I sent a couple of easy questions to six of our city’s candidates from the two major parties. It’s fair to say that the North has been economically ripped off for more than 15 years. How will you change this? Are you willing to vote against your party to benefit your region?

The LNP candidates didn’t respond. Possibly they are adopting a small-target strategy, as if they are shoe-ins on January 31. It must feel good to be that confident.

The Labor candidates responded, indicating they would raise local issues in their party room. They also seem to be curiously void of new ideas for the

North, having flushed up some old policy of an assistant minister for North Queensland. Like the title second capital of Queensland, this thought bubble is as useless as an ejection seat in a helicopter.

Remember, Labor, while previously in power, pillaged billions from the North and spent it on southern infrastructure. Labor needs to seek economic forgiveness from the North before they throw "Our Fair Share" grenades at the current Government. But the current Government needs to share the proceeds of the North's hard work better than they have in their first term.

This election is not just about economic management, public debt, asset leases and an economically unconvincing stadium; it's about Townsville jobs, confidence, competitively priced baseload power for the North, our environment, state stamp duty on home insurance and the cost of living in the North. With respect, LNP and ALP, you can both do better!

This election is about our courageous candidates representing us in Brisdrain and reducing their representation of their party in the North. Finally, the worst possible outcome for Townsville after this state election is to have three MPs who are not members of the victorious party. The stadium will be delayed, confidence will remain low and drawn out, unacceptably high unemployment will continue and population growth will suffer.

In this column, I reveal after a short investigation that KAP actually hold more seats than any other party in North Queensland. They are the NQ opposition, with loads of opportunity and political influence.

Stand up KAP, you're the Opposition

Words: 378

THE Queensland Electoral Commission website has some interesting statistics on the 2012 state election.

The most interesting of all is that the Katter's Australian Party came second in Northern Queensland and effectively holds the title of "the Opposition" in and around Townsville.

I suppose the question is will this be maintained at the next election?

The northern zone comprises six state electorates.

Five are held by Liberal National Party members and one by Katter's Australian Party.

But most telling of all is that while the conservatives won 42 per cent of the vote and Katter's Australian Party won 33 per cent, only 21 per cent was won by Labor.

This means that three quarters of the population in the northern zone rejected the Labor Party.

Like the federal election, only 5 per cent was won by the Greens, indicating a huge reduction in support for their candidates and policy.

Why was this?

Well there was a vibe for change, a new and vibrant conservative leader and the Labor Party was seen as being out of touch with its support base on delivering our fair share and selling assets.
It's never about one variable and there may well be more but the Labor leader was also on the nose.
Will this northern voting phenomenon remain?
It's hard to predict.
Last election many traditional Labor voters deserted the party.
But they couldn't bring themselves to vote for the conservatives, so they decided to vote for the Katter party.
It's likely that some of those disillusioned Labor voters will return to traditional voting patterns, especially since Katter's Australian Party has been quiet leading into this election.
With about 70 per cent of the state seats held by LNP, it's a fair call that the conservatives should retain government.
While the conservative leader has had some of his shine knocked off, essentially the northern Opposition leader, or leader of Katter's Australian Party is not in the same popularity league.
KAP may well pick up northern Queensland seats at the next state election and so too may Labor, but the conservatives should retain power in Queensland.
As the opposition in Northern Queensland, we need to see KAPs policy's for northern economic recovery and resilience.
What is their policy to achieve Our Fair Share?

My political columns develop depth and structure of Our Fair share concept and method. Combined with economic data they are powerful tools.

4 ECONOMIC COLUMNS

Over the decades I've provided my economic opinion to national, state and local media sources for free. It's a way of promoting the value of my profession, encouraging public scrutiny of our tax dollars (keeping the bastards honest) and supporting my community. Over the years ive been told that I have influenced many younger people to study economics at University. I'm happy with my positive diversified contribution.

Economic based columns of Our Fair Share collection comprised the majority articles; around 40% of all columns. They are the foundation of Our Fair Share and fundamental for other section of the method.

The following Our Fair Share essay is my first Economic column. There is political change federally. I suggest prosecuting harder and smarter to achieve better cut through. "*Too much attention is being given to the archaic and high-cost car industry in Victoria and South Australia. Canberra should be looking north for fresh innovative and positive economic* *development. Australia needs industrious cities that get on with the job of prosperity, that will drive consistent population growth, create jobs and bolster the integrated supply chain.*

Townsville is that sort of positive diversified city that contributes, but we want our fair share of public expenditure."

I call the capital by its real name and not Cantberra.

Shout loud to help our region prosper

Words: 344

THE year ahead is shaping up as a promising economic period for Townsville but we need loud voices to reduce some challenges ahead and ensure we obtain our fair share.

In 2014 the combined northern and northwest economic activity is likely to hit the $20 billion GRP mark but Townsville's economic horizon for 2014 has many challenges. If we look hard there are opportunities, but we need our fair share from federal and state governments to consolidate sustainable economic growth, retain and create new jobs, and progress towards becoming Australia's leading regional city. The largest city in Northern Australia is struggling under the weight of rising unemployment, falling job creation and falling participation levels. The region requires a multidimensional, innovative solution that combines state and federal capital and recurrent expenditure injections with private sector innovation. We have to go fishing for the solution rather than wait for it to jump into the boat.

As a leading Australian regional city with a resilient and well integrated economy, Townsville's private sector needs to think outside the square to progress its comparative advantage. Townsville needs to take advantage of a depreciating currency and develop an image makeover, prosecute (whinge) harder for better public investment injections and encourage smart new leaders to forge new industries. We also need to look outside our region to the Pacific and Asia to take advantage of our proximity and products we can provide to our neighbours.

In May, the new Federal Government will deliver its first Budget. If current federal political rhetoric is any indicator, Townsville can expect a tough time. Too much attention is being given to the archaic and high-cost car industry in Victoria and South Australia. Canberra should be looking north for fresh innovative and positive economic development. Australia needs industrious cities that get on with the job of prosperity, that will drive consistent population growth, create jobs and bolster the integrated supply chain.

Townsville is that sort of positive diversified city that contributes, but we want our fair share of public expenditure.

Colin Dwyer is a Townsville-based economist.

In this economic OFS essay I look to economic history and provide a vision for the future. Not just five or ten years, I'm thinking two generations. That's the vision consistent with Our Fair Share and enduring economic stability. I let the reader know that Townsville has had tough economic times in the past and describes the reason. I argue for efficient and affordable baseload power, without this, Townsville's future is modest and mendicant. There's lots of future election material in this column. This was the best headline I got – Voice of the North.

Voice of the North Dreaming up a plan

Words: 567

AS the 50th anniversary of Martin Luther King's famous ``I have a Dream" speech approaches, it's time to reflect on the progress Townsville has made in the past fifty years and where we dream to be in 2063. I have a dream.

Fifty years ago Townsville was an outpost of Australian society.

Stuck away in the oppressive, jobless north there was little reason to migrate to Townsville. Since then much has changed.

Rewind 50 years and for Townsville the '60s and '70s belonged to mining, defence and education. Similar to the noughties, manufacturing, services to mining in the northwest and defence expenditure dominated gross regional product.

In the '60s, Townsville port was bustling with defence ships heading to Vietnam and shipping minerals to fuel Japan's rising economy. Yabulu and the copper refineries opened their doors.

Economically the '80s and '90s were consolidating periods. Sun Metals was lured with cheap land and guaranteed water supply and the Burdekin Dam provided water security for northern Queensland.

Townsville's population grew consistently but it was slow and net migration in some periods, such a 1996-7, was negative, due to federal government public sector cuts.

Construction and the housing sector were stagnant, unemployment was high and inflation was strong as the Aussie dollar dipped.

After 40 years of diversified growth Townsville experienced a once-in-a-generation boom fuelled by defence, mining and indirectly by construction.

Townsville is a city that attracts residents by its ability to provide jobs. As APS job-shedding approaches, mining jobs are lost and unemployment creeps higher, Townsville's reputation as a low-risk regional investment opportunity is likely to take some flack. But Townsville is a remarkably resilient economy in a regional location, as the past 50 years tells us.

Fast forward 50 years and the population of Townsville could be between 450,000 and 550,000, 70,000 more than Canberra now.

But for this to happen some major economic events need to occur. These events need to be game changers and diversification additions. We need facilities to support 300,000 more residents and 150,000 new jobs.

The major facility that Townsville needs is a baseload power station that supplies affordable and efficient power.

The combination of competitive power supply, cheap abundant land and water, skilled workers and proximity to Asia would drive the regional economy.

Developing the vast northern interior for agriculture to feed the growing masses of Asia would create thousands of direct and indirect jobs. It may require the raising of the Burdekin dam wall, The defence force is likely to expand in the next 50 years. The army barracks could move to an isolated location.

More residential land could be opened up.

The port could relocate its main services to Cape Cleveland as maxi ships dominate the seas.

Refineries, encouraged by affordable power, abundant cheap water and cheap land could be built south of Townsville.

Our technological systems need to grow and we need to be at the forefront of new age computing.

In 50 years the Constitution should have changed to reflect the population distribution of growing Australia.

Northern Queensland as a regional powerhouse will have at least one member in the Senate and North Queensland will have three or four. The Lower House representation will increase from one to two or three.

Yes I have a dream; an optimistic, positive dream. The dream is of political equity, fiscal distribution equity and social equity. Where the federal and state budgets provide ``Our Fair Share", and health, aged care and education standards are as good as the national benchmark.

Comparatively higher Insurance costs have been a continuing issue in North Queensland since Cyclone Larry and Yasi. I spent weeks of personal time researching and advocating for better insurance outcomes for Northerners. I was the first to point out that northerners pay more on average for home insurance and if they pay more than southerners then northerners pay more State tax (GST and Stamp Duty). This issue is eventually investigated and ratified by the ACCC, years later. Eventually, I present two submissions to their inquiries and complete a free economic impact study in 2019. No solution currently exists as of 2020.

Costs analysis merely skims surface

Words: 419

ACCORDING to a State Government report Townsville is the cheapest place to live in North Queensland. When Queensland treasury compared a variety of products in July and August 2013, a Townsville basket of goods was cheaper than similar items in Cairns, Mackay and even Brisbane.

The report shows Townsville to be 1.6 per cent cheaper than Greater Brisbane. Transport costs were 6.3 per cent cheaper but furnishings and household equipment were 11 per cent dearer than in Brisbane.

Interestingly the insurance component was only 2.9 per cent dearer than in Brisbane in 2013.

This sparked my interest because I know friends and family who pay three times less for insurance in Greater Brisbane than I do.

But it's not what they've included – it's what they've excluded that makes me question the relevance of the report.

Collecting this data is a tough job and rather than answering our comparative cost of living questions it merely begs the question: Why aren't we included in the quarterly ABS CPI figures? If it's worth doing, it's worth doing properly.

Firstly home insurance is excluded from this survey. They include contents and comprehensive vehicle insurance.

Home insurance is a state election issue and a key household budget item in North Queensland.

It needs to be included in any cost of living survey.

Secondly the report is a snapshot of 2013 conditions and is not comparable to previous reports. How do we measure the change that has occurred since the previous report in 2011 or the reports before that?

Then there are the fuel figures obtained in 2013 when Townsville prices were cheaper than Brisbane's.

But only 12 months previously we had a 20 per cent more expensive price than Brisbane's fuel costs.
More regular reports are needed. Every two years is not acceptable.
Also we are not comparing similar regions. The Brisbane base area is a combination of five local government authorities. Why not geographic catchments or population catchment price comparisons? If we used Brisbane LGA as the base region they would look unaffordable and expensive.
This report offers some good insights to how Townsville Rockhampton, Cairns and Mackay retail prices compare to Greater Brisbane. But it doesn't allow us to measure change or allow us to compare some important household budget items that are hurting North Queensland family budgets. This report adds weight to the call for Townsville, the largest city in North Australia, to be included in the ABS quarterly CPI. Please j oin the CPI for North Queensland campaign: http://chn.ge/PsdnY4

This column highlights the reason why I got involved in economic advocacy and politics. The essay discusses the 2014 state budget and regional capital investment or state public investment.

Region has missed out on due wealth
Words: 409

MORE than 10 years ago I noticed local politicians were thanking the Brisbane-based State Government for all they were doing with their State Budget. They were claiming Brisbane was providing ample capital investment for the north. I decided to launch a fact check into their claims and I found them to be unfounded.

I have been gathering relevant state public investment data since 2000 and in that time have provided a consistent approach to calculating Our Fair Share. I hope I avoid the floccinaucinihilipilification.

The Our Fair Share formula involves population share, population growth and economic contribution and growth. Greater Townsville has 5 per cent of state population, above average population growth and 4 per cent of GSP. I weight these variables in my Our Fair Share formula.

According to Budget paper 3 appendix C the 2014-15 state public investment in the Townsville region is the best "Our Fair Share" we have seen since 2000.

Greater Townsville received $26 million more capital expenditure than last year and 7.3 per cent of this year's capital budget.

This is in a capital expenditure budget that receded $1.6 billion around the state. The region expects to receive $675.9 million state public investment in the next financial year.

With Greater Townsville's unemployment at 8.4 per cent, persistently low business and consumer confidence, and residential construction below long-run averages we need public capital injections, consistent public sector jobs and private sector innovation.

In capital expenditure terms, roads are our big winner followed by energy and water. My economic crystal ball can see more roadworks leading up to the next state election, which in my opinion won't be until after the G20 leaders meeting in Brisbane on November 15 and 16.

Disappointing parts of the State Budget include local education investment, especially given the number of babies being born in the region and current comparative Naplan results. I am discouraged by the comments about sale of the port, frustrated with the lack of attention given to home insurance challenges for the 350,000 voters north of the Fitzroy, and unsatisfied with the cost of living pressures being placed on pensioners.

Overall it was a solid State Budget that reduces debt and deficits but was too optimistic about the doubling of economic growth to 6 per cent next year. Greater Townsville and the rest of North Queensland deserves its fair share of public investment and has earned the right to consistent accuracy in the claims of politicians.

I received significant positive feedback from this column.... *Complex challenges like home insurance are never based on a silver bullet solution. We need a silver buckshot solution*

managing the multiple challenges in this failing market to develop a sustainable solution for north Queensland families. **In this column I use a term I created in 2006 – <u>Silver Buckshot Solution</u>, it means a diversified solution. Journalists constantly look for the silver bullet problem and singular solution; they know readers are likely to have differing opinions. I think it diminishes journalism when they do this.**

I would regularly attend public forums and contribute important information that could help the whole community. Home insurance was a significant issue and I made this point at ABC national Forum held in Townsville. I made several recommendations in the following essay some of which have been adopted by decision makers - *In addition concessions should be available for flood free and cyclone rated homes.*

The ACCC released its second report into Northern Home insurance in late December 2019, close to Christmas. I completed a DRAFT estimated economic impact that was used in a Courier Mail story. The ACCC had over 20 recommendations, in July 2020 none had been ratified by the federal government. Has it fallen off the table? Have higher disparate insurance premiums and northerners paying way more state tax become accepted?

Fixing insurance failure a vote winner

Words: 465

AT an ABC national forum in Townsville the presenter asked the group "is there any issue that would make you change the way you vote?".

I put my hand up and said if someone could fix home insurance I would vote for them.

The home insurance solution in the North involves state and federal governments working together with private sector to solve market failure and reduce state stamp duties, manage commissions and standardise home insurance for all Australians.

Today's State Budget needs to give back our fair share to the North, improve Northern cost of living pressures on families and reduce stamp duty on home insurance for all North Queensland. Complex challenges like home insurance are never based on a silver bullet solution. We need a silver buckshot approach managing the multiple challenges in this failing market to develop a sustainable solution for north Queensland families.

Not only can the state provide concessions on stamp duty for northerners, because we already give so much in mining royalties and pay relatively more for a similar house, they can also act to reduce the commission that agents receive.

Before 2011 the commission was set by the state at 20 per cent. The average northern home paid a similar total home insurance amount to other

Australian households in the vicinity of $1000 to $1500 per year.

Since 2011, individual home insurance has increased to around $3300 per annum. About 20 per cent of this fee goes to the selling agent. There are more than 350,000 homes in North Queensland and about 500,000 voters.

The state can manage the commission of agents much better, such as adopting a flat fee or sliding scale rate rather than a percentage commission. For example $300 per annum for each home indexed to the consumer price index or building cost index seems relatively fair.

In addition concessions should be available for flood free and cyclone rated homes.

This puts an added burden on those that aren't in this category but others have already paid a structural and land fee to build more structurally sound flood free homes.

Finally the Federal Government should standardise home insurance premiums so we all share the burden of natural disasters.

Sharing the burden of home insurance reduces our costs; increases southern costs marginally but in the long run makes Australia a fairer place to live.

The solution to our home insurance problem is a silver buckshot approach with state taking 30 per cent responsibility (stamp duty and commissions), federal taking 50 per cent responsibility (market standardisation) and the private sector taking 20 per cent responsibility (competition/profit).

The Federal Government needs to provide a Consumer Price Index for Townsville so we can monitor household budget price changes.
We the consumer need to stand up and fight for this change.

Insurance hasn't gone away and I am still contributing new evidence to the discussion. In this essay I 'keep the bastards honest with my reference to increase in stamp duty costs, northerners paying more because of this and the unfaithfulness of the new treasurer. Recent stamp duty changes have added a further 1.5 per cent in stamp duty on insurance premiums, up from 7.5 per cent to 9 per cent. This financial year, state government coffers are estimated to grow by over $800 million from stamp duty on insurance alone. That is projected to swell to over $1 billion by 2015-16.
There is a triple impact on people of North Queensland, we pay more for our houses, more for insurance stamp duty and then you collect even more from us with a GST on the higher construction costs and increased stamp duty; compounding the state tax burden on families north of the Fitzroy. When he was on the Opposition benches, Treasurer Tim Nicholls called insurance duty a "windfall on misery". Now in government, you are perpetuating this inconsistency. Why would northerners vote for or support such deceitful madness?

Time to act on insurance, Mr Premier
Words: 431

WELCOME back to Townsville Mr Premier. We appreciate your time in the largest city in North Australia. From Rockhampton north to the Torres Strait we are sick of paying higher home insurance fees than the south and the Queensland Government needs to remove or reduce stamp duty on all property insurance in North Queensland in next week's state budget.

North Queensland Insurance premiums have skyrocketed since natural disasters in 2011-12. Since these disasters we have seen home insurance hikes in the order of 300 to 800 per cent. This places unnecessary and unfair burdens on those people living in North Queensland. In a signal of market failure some insurance companies won't take new insurance business.

State Government stamp duty changes have placed an extra burden on northerners and we are paying more than our fair share of state taxes. Recent stamp duty changes have added a further 1.5 per cent in stamp duty on insurance premiums, up from 7.5 per cent to 9 per cent. This financial year, state government coffers are estimated to grow by over $800 million from stamp duty on insurance alone. That is projected to swell to over $1 billion by 2015-16.

To cope with our weather conditions, we have taken it upon ourselves to build structurally responsible but more expensive homes without due recognition from Brisbane or insurance companies. Most homes in Townsville have been built with a cyclone rating (a form of insurance) that increases building costs by around 30 per cent compared to southern homes. There is a triple impact on people of North Queensland, we pay more for our houses, more for insurance stamp duty and then you collect even more from us with a GST on the extra construction costs and increased stamp duty; compounding the state tax burden on families north of the Fitzroy.

When he was on the Opposition benches, Treasurer Tim Nicholls called insurance duty a “windfall on misery”. Now in government, you are perpetuating this inconsistency.

The North is arguably one of the most productive regions in Australia. We contribute significantly to state revenue via mining royalties, GST, stamp duty, Port and Ergon revenue and payroll tax.

The home insurance disaster in the North is not just a federal government issue. The solution involves state and federal governments working together with the private sector to solve market failure and remove or reduce state stamp duties. In next week’s state budget give back to the North, improve Northern affordability and cost of living pressures on families and reduce or remove stamp duty on home insurance for all North Queensland.

In the next article I simplify the relationship between politics and economics with..

"Classic three-year politics is to shock, smooth and bribe the electorate. In the first year tell them the bad news and make it sound worse than it is – remember the banana republic comment from Paul Keating. The second year is spent consoling the electorate and making them feel better, building confidence along the way. The final year is about bribing key electorates to get back in for another three years."

It's a good description of a complex political strategy after a party has just won power after being in opposition for a long time.

Fantasy economics had to be halted

Words: 367

LAST year's federal Budget (2013-14) was written by a 'Pollyanna', someone suffering from illogical optimism. Its assumptions were formulated in economic fantasyland and it needed fixing. This year's Budget turned a corner. Welcome to the politics of budget renovation and federation wedging.

Australia has just seen the toughest federal Budget since 1997, with spending cut and taxes raised to generate savings not seen for the better part of two decades.

And now we wait and see if the states will drive the agenda to change the GST to fill an $80 billion health and education fiscal void.

The GST was introduced by the Howard Government and commenced on July 1, 2000, replacing the previous federal wholesale sales tax and designed to phase out a number of various state and territory government taxes, duties and levies such as banking taxes and stamp duty. If the GST is to change all the state parliaments and two federal houses need to agree.

The recent change in federal funding for education and health seems to be a strategy by the Federal Government to wedge the states into agreement to change GST. This change could come in two forms; an increase in the rate, currently 10 per cent, or the inclusion of fresh food in the tax, currently exempt.

There's an additional challenge north of the Tweed River.

Queensland goes to the polls within 12 months and brings an election budget down next month.

The loss of billions to the state budget is surely a blow to the revenue side of an election budget.

Classic three-year politics is to shock, smooth and bribe the electorate. In the first year tell them the bad news and make it sound worse than it is – remember the banana republic comment from Paul Keating. The second year is spent consoling the

electorate and making them feel better, building confidence along the way.
The final year is about bribing key electorates to get back in for another three years.
The Townsville region, with six state seats, has its fair share of key electorates and needs a fiscal injection to boost confidence, drive the economy and build the largest most diversified city north of the Sunshine Coast.

In this column I refer to how the northern mining boom saved the national budget from enduring deficits and, created surpluses. Im frustrated that southerns have forgotten our contribution so quickly. I also reinforce my three year economic-poltical cycle theory with this in the first year – *we have to clean up, there's a shocking financial mess*!! I point out *This economic medicine is a bitter pill to swallow for northerners. It looks like Canberra has forgotten the north's contribution through the mining boom.*

Razor gang back with a vengeance
Words: 416

REMEMBER the days when the Budget had more money than it could poke a stick at? For almost a decade, the Coalition pulled bigger than expected surpluses out of the magic budget hat and we all enjoyed pension boosts, baby bonuses, extra family payments and tax cuts. We lived like there were no more tough economic times tomorrow.

Unfortunately the Coalition government blew it with handouts to win consecutive elections, and Labor spent the rest on the GFC bailout and other more unworthy programs. It's a sorry fact that we've managed to come through the biggest mining boom since gold rush days with little to show for it. Now we are faced with an empty cup and it's cracked.

Last year's final Labor budget was based on exaggerated economic numbers and fantasy land economic growth figures just so we could be seen to afford Gillard's massive spending spree.

In office for one year before the GFC, Labor failed to rein in the worst of the Howard government's budget excesses. It introduced a carbon tax that cost more in compensation than it raised. It poorly designed a mining tax that raised little revenue but had plenty of big spending promises attached. Worthy social policies like a National Disability Insurance Scheme and the Gonski education funding boost were never fully funded.

Corrective action to fix Labor's economic incompetence is required and apparently we all have to chip in. This economic medicine is a bitter pill to swallow for northerners. It looks like Canberra has forgotten the north's contribution through the mining boom. But let's see what comes of the Northern Development Committee report.

There are three structural cracks in Australia's Budget left by a receding mining boom, an ageing population and expensive new social policies. On the expenditure side of the Budget, I expect we'll have to forget about tax cuts and bonus welfare cheques for a long time and we'll all be working longer before we get the pension. On the revenue side, bracket creep will do much of the hard work as the average wage earner in seven to ten years will likely be paying a mean tax rate of 28 cents in the dollar up from 23 per cent. Prepare to pay more to visit the GP and receive fewer family tax benefits as the Coalition wields the knife. The razor gang is back and unfortunately we are going to contribute more than our fair share for some time. Let's hope Canberra remembers our contribution.

Affordable, reliable and sustainable baseload power has been a long term challenge for North Queensland. The current coal fired based system for north Queensland is located in Gladstone and there is no national grid connection to the north West Mineral province. In this essay I ask the question Should we be considering Nuclear energy to solve our power, affordability and CO2 trilemma?

Analysis adds insight to nuclear issue

Words: 399

THE uranium mining debate is healthy and alive and it's important we discuss the nuclear opportunity maturely and consider all the related challenges.

Townsville and the rest of North Queensland need an affordable baseload power-generation system and Townsville has a lower-grade uranium deposit within its boundaries, Ben Lomond.

Should we be mining it? A simple PESTEL analysis may help, providing factual information on Political, Economic, Social, Technological, Environmental and Legal issues associated with a project.

Politically, the State Government will soon allow uranium mining again in Queensland. This is a key step to this issue. We also know there's a state election occurring within one year. Is the current debate analytical or politically motivated?

Economically, Ben Lomond is not comparatively high grade. There are other mines in the North West mineral province that have better-grade uranium. They are also relatively isolated and unlikely to directly affect waterways and populations of humans and animals.

Exporting the product is a challenge but there are three transport options: Darwin, Karumba or Townsville. Is transporting uranium ore safe if it is exported through Townsville? How many jobs will be created? Is the benefit cost ratio positive and high?

Socially, there may be health challenges with uranium extraction and tailings but any new mine has stringent and comprehensive rules and any application must consider these issues.

Technologically, we need to collect evidence and analyse what advances have been made in safe uranium extraction and transport from the South Australian and Canadian experiences.

Environmentally, each mine – whether it be a coal mine or uranium mine – has to be cleared through comprehensive environmental guidelines before it can proceed. Ben Lomond would be scrutinised rigorously to assess the risks and benefits from such a venture.

Ben Lomond is a lower-grade uranium deposit that would need the correct economic, political, social and environmental variables to get approval. Other mines would be better placed to start uranium mining in North Queensland.

Economists don't just analyse the commercial viability of a project, they seek the whole truth. We're not lawyers but we consider the legal obligations. We're not environmentalists but we consider the externalities in a project. Most importantly, economists argue for our fair share, whether it be public or private investment, environmental sustainability or community wellbeing.

Economics is about helping current and future generations make positive decisions; politics is about framing issues and wedging or dividing voters.

In this economic OFS essay I investigate specific Local government economics and challenge a specific project to produce better results. The Kissing Point development had

been a long term challenge that exemplified the difficulty different levels of government and parties have in committing to a project. At the time the conservatives were in power federally, the progressives held the state and local government. Kissing Point was a federally owned piece of land that was being offered back to the local community if the state and local contributed a third each to the project. It was a classic frame and wedge situation that stalled the project and frustrated local residents and voters. In the end many voters turned to minor parties that had regional interests as their core value.

How we just kissed goodbye to $40m
Words: 376

I WENT for a walk around Jezzine Barracks redevelopment recently.
It's a wonderful addition to the lifestyle assets of Townsville.
I think the board has done a worthy job sometimes under challenging circumstances. But $40 million!
Don't get me wrong I think Kissing Point is great, but it's just not worth a whopping $40 million. To put it in perspective, the three kilometres of Strand with buildings and groins officially cost $28 million

back in 1998, which in current dollars is about $80 million; two times more than Kissing Point cost.

I don't believe Kissing Point is anywhere near half as good as the Strand, but is it a model that delivers our fair share?

When I look at the Kissing Point facilities I can't see $40 million – there is no substantial building, just landscaping, walkways, boardwalks and sculptures.

I understand there were contamination issues and that it cost a lot to mitigate these challenges.

I also understand that disability access costs a significant amount.

But I'm struggling with the price tag of $40 million; and for half the official Strand development cost when calculated in current dollars.

If you had $40 million to spend on Townsville facilities would you have spent it on Jezzine? Hypothetically, for what we got, I would have spent $20 million on Kissing Point redevelopment and not a cent more.

Given that the residual $20 million would have stayed in Townsville, I would have upgraded other facilities.

The convention centre would have got some and 1300 Smiles stadium would have got some. When you maintain existing facilities you usually get a more productive outcome than building a new facility.

Anything left over would have been contestable.

Kissing Point is a wonderful lifestyle addition to Townsville, but it is way too expensive for what we got.

While I would have spent the money differently, I have come to the only logical conclusion that this is how projects are built down south.
So maybe I should be thankful for a wonderful facility, be happy about all the local jobs that were created and satisfied with all the local businesses that benefited. I accept that at least with this facility we got our fair share and we should enjoy this fantastic new venue.

This is a classic economic Our Fair Share essay, updated from my 2008 essay, comparing North Queensland to Tasmania.

Equal treatment tops policy wish list

Words: 346

THE Constitution is an archaic inflexible piece of governance that needs to be challenged and reformed. The constitution supports a political gerrymander that influences public sector investment and favours states far more than regions; which in my opinion is obsolete and needs reforming. The disparity in political representation between North Queensland and Tasmania is profound, inequitable and un-Australian. As Australia's leading regional city Townsville needs to scrutinise and challenge this legislated inequity and encourage robust debate.

Back in 1901 Tasmania had more residents than North Queensland and they became a state. That's fine, but 113 years on, Australian population distribution and regional economic contribution have changed. Today the constitution supports a gerrymander of massive proportions. Tasmania with 352,203 voters (and zero population growth) has five MPs. North of the Fitzroy there's also five MPs but 30 per cent more voters than Tasmania and much faster population growth.

Unfortunately the gerrymander is compounded as the composition of the senate makes a mockery of democracy. North of the Fitzroy there's one senator for 250,000 voters compared with Tasmania's one is to 29,000. Yes that's one senator for every 29,000 voters – that's fewer voters electing a federal senator in Tasmania than voters electing a state member in Queensland! Tasmania effectively has nine times better representation in the senate than North Queensland and can effectively have more influence on public investment decisions. Tasmania has 17 representatives in Canberra and North Queensland seven.

The North has taken the current federal system of representation for granted but, comparative population, political and economic evidence suggests it's time to challenge the system's integrity. NQ has a population larger than Tasmania and the Northern Territory and an economy that dwarfs both Tasmania and the NT and is almost equal to South Australia. Yet North Queensland's federal representation is vastly diminished.

If democracy occurs where all eligible citizens participate equally, then Townsville, North Queensland and other parts of the country need constitutional reform that supports fairer representation for all Australians. We need reform that reflects contemporary Australia and delivers our fair share of public investment.

In the next OFS essay I reveal that Townsville is not just the largest city in North Australia but if you draw a line from Noosa to Adelaide and cap off Perth there's a big parcel of Australia left where Townsville has a big leadership role.

Speak up to get fair share of budget
Words: 369

IN 2014, Townsville looks forward to consistent population growth and moving closer to becoming the 12th-largest Australian city. Indeed if you draw a line from Noosa to Adelaide the land mass to the west and north of that line accounts for more than 80 per cent of Australia and Townsville is the second largest city in that area behind Perth. Soon Townsville will have 200,000 residents.

This population benchmark is a major event in Townsville's progress and we need a committee to celebrate our city cracking the 200,000 residents mark.

But there is some concern about our population growth. If the Federal Government significantly reduces the public sector payroll in the May budget,

Townsville's economy could suffer. Already a centre of health services, this industry could be cut substantially to help pay for the debt burden of previous governments. Similar to 1997 Townsville could experience a negative net migration as Australian public servants are made redundant.

As the Federal Government is making budget decisions now, we need a strong voice around the decision table that disagrees with this approach as history suggests this approach would deepen the current economic wound in Townsville. The impact of Australian Public Service redundancy's on the local economy 16 years ago was harsh as retail suffered, property prices stagnated, vacancy rates soared and our investment advantages diminished.

We already have substantial challenges with our wider workforce performing below long run averages, unemployment rates stagnating and participation rates falling. Governments need to invest in our region, creating new jobs, supporting a region that has given more per person over the past decade than many other regions.

Townsville is trending positively towards being Australia's leading regional city but we need our fair share from Brisbane and Canberra. If we have maintained a consistent 2.4 per cent population growth since 2012 Townsville's population is currently about 191,413 and set to crack the 200,000 towards the end of 2015 or early 2016.

We need a committee to provide an audit of current infrastructure assets and deficiencies for a regional city with 200,000 residents. We also need to pop our cork, put on the LBD or tux, and tell the rest of Australia we're celebrating 200,000 residents in 2016.

In this next essay I provide important, previously unknown evidence, about North Queensland. I am developing a foundation for future articles and recommendations.

In need of more effective economics

Words: 370

OUR region is a prosperous area but we need our fair share of public investment and recurrent funding to build our prosperity. It's time the wider Townsville region started using the combination of the Northern and the North-West statistical divisions as its geographical boundaries for economic contribution calculations and prosecuted for better economic development infrastructure and supporting services. The combined Northern and North-West regions are likely to set a new economic benchmark in 2014 – $20 billion Gross Regional Product.

There are many good reasons to adopt this new measure of economic activity. Firstly, the economic links with Mount Isa are consistent and abundant with mining and agriculture products being exported through the Townsville Port.

Secondly, there are thousands of FIFO workers who use Townsville as their base, use the facilities in Townsville but work in North-West division. Each region depends on the other for economic production; it's an economic symbiosis.

Finally, the Far North has an area more than three times the Northern region; it makes comparative economic and geographical sense to combine Northern and North-West regions when we describe the wider Townsville economic activity, contribution and demographics.

Northern and North-West workers contribute at a higher rate than the rest of Queensland (18.7 per cent) and Australia (11.5 per cent). According to the latest OESR Gross Regional Product figures and allowing for 3 per cent economic growth, the Northern and North-West regions contribute about $7 billion, or 35 per cent, more than the Far North, with a similar population.

On average, each individual in the Northern and North-West divisions contributes $71,429, while each Tasmanian contributes only $45,000.

Our region has many pressing needs and a vision for our future. We urgently need an infrastructure audit followed by cost-effective base load power generated closer to our region.

We need better public investment such as a new stadium, or an iconic art building. The numeracy and literacy levels of the next generation of northerners are below state and national benchmarks; we need urgent action in this area.

The private sector's push into southwest Asia and the Pacific needs to be better supported. We need our fair share of public investment and recurrent expenditure to achieve better jobs and an improved lifestyle.

In this OFS essay I point out that smaller centres such as Mt Isa and Darwin have a Grocery Price index why not north Australia's largest city, Townsville. The ABS could provide it.

I conducted a Townsville Grocery Price Survey for several years, created a unique regional grocery price Index and also advocated for fair petrol prices in Townsville and Cairns and across North Queensland.

Families living expenses are a powerful economic and political lever.

This city warrants independent CPI
Words: 375

TOWNSVILLE, the largest city in North Australia, deserves an official quarterly CPI. Darwin has a quarterly CPI with 75,000 fewer people and Cairns and Mt Isa had a quarterly grocery price index, but amusingly it was produced by the Northern Territory Government.
Northern Queensland is experiencing unique cost pressures different to the findings in the latest CPI report. In 2013, northern households felt the burden of significant price rises and/or differences for home insurance, petrol prices and energy costs.

The major summary of national inflation data didn't comment on any of these items as significantly increasing cost to all Australian consumers. Nationally insurance costs have increased only marginally, electricity prices are stable and fuel prices have had little impact on household budgets — completely different to our experience.

One can only assume that these particular rising prices are North Queensland issues?

Our electricity prices and home insurance costs have soared recently as a consequence of carbon tax, gold plated infrastructure and apparently unique weather events. Well we can't reverse the construction standards but we can abolish the carbon tax. But as for unique weather events that destroy homes and increase insurance costs, Brisbane has floods, Sydney has tornadoes and Canberra, Melbourne, Hobart, Adelaide and Perth bushfires. So why is North Queensland paying a higher price for home insurance?

Why isn't the price variation between metropolitan and regional cities being officially monitored?

It's not just price increases that need official monitoring, we need comparative price monitoring of individual products.

Townsville motorists have noticed a slight increase in the price of ULP in December from around 153c/litre to 156c/litre with a 2.7c lower average price than Brisbane. But last year there was a massive 20 cent per ULP litre higher price in Townsville than Brisbane. Such irregularities are

worth investigating. Something's not right in the petrol market!
As the largest city in North Australia Townsville needs a consistent, official and comparable consumer price index that informs Canberra and Brisbane as much as local businesses, unions and families about our unique market conditions.
This way policy makers can make informed decisions that consider North Queenslanders, compare price variations and, when market irregularities occur, act to protect and help North Queenslanders prosper and continue to contribute our fair share.

In this next OFS essay I provide important economic information about Townsville and identify Townsville's more 'resilient locations'. Good information for any budding economist or investor. With months until a state election I reach out to opposition and minor parties for their plan for Townsville. These plans never eventuated because neither minor or labor expected to win – yet they did. The ALP plan for Townsville region is finally being developed before the 2020 state election.

Region deserves realistic proposals

Words: 358

THERE'S more than one way to catch a coral trout. Just as there is more than one way to achieve better economic development, and, with a state election looming, now is not the time to play the unrealistic optimistic pollyanna card.

By all means be positive but we need to accept our challenges far more than we have and prosecute the case for more government spending in our region.

On the other side of the ledger, governments need to acknowledge our contribution, and together we need to focus on how we are going to build a more resilient economy.

Our economic compass needs several captains who understand our challenges and opportunities; people who will fearlessly engage the political minefield and extract quality sustainable public pots of gold, while boosting our brand and encouraging new business opportunities and creating sustainable jobs.

We have about four to six months to let all the political parties know that we have contributed over the years and we want, need and demand our long-run fair share of fiscal election injection. Basically, we know the first part of the LNP package and their solution.

What we would like to know is if Labor has a plan for Townsville.

If the smaller parties and independents gain control of the State Parliament what is their plan for Townsville?

Over the coming weeks I will reveal Townsville "battlerburbs" – suburbs that are in jobs crisis – and our "resilitburbs" – those suburbs that have consistently low unemployment.

Our challenge as a city is to reinforce these battlerburbs with new sustainable regional industries, while building on our economic strengths and cleverly restructuring the economy and brand of the largest city in North Australia.

Townsville is experiencing a three-speed economy.

This description of Townsville is supported by recent small area labour force data for June 2014, released by Department of Employment, which reveals those Townsville suburbs that are experiencing jobs crisis, those in urgent need of attention and those that are resilient in these tough economic times.

The time has come for Labor, other parties and independents to reveal their solutions for the Townsville region.

Next Week: Townsville's battlerburbs.

In this OFS essay published before Christmas 2013 I reveal some of Townsville's economic strengths and resilient suburbs. Writing these essays requires sound sources of evidence.

Assets a solid foundation for our city

Words: 422

I HOPE you enjoy a positive day with your family on Thursday. For me Christmas is about family because it's our families that support us in tough times and enjoy life with us in the good. Townsville is a unique collection of strong, diverse and vulnerable families.

Like our families, Townsville's economy has some solid performing and resilient components.

Sometimes our greater family gets blasé about its positive achievements and quality assets such as the largest army barracks in Australia, largest sugar and base metals port in Australia, largest regional hospital in Queensland, significant tertiary education assets that other regional centres would like to have in their portfolio and, of course, the title of largest city in North Australia.

All these components mean Townsville has assets that provide a solid foundation to help our community achieve its full potential and hopefully have some fun along the way. Townsville's many resilient suburbs reinforce this solid foundation, especially when it comes to jobs.

Families are great to confide in and they are great to get a pep talk about overcoming challenges. Our unemployment rate, while unacceptably high, is not as bad as it may seem. Townsville City's unemployment rate is lower than the regional rate due to poor performing outer cities and towns. The higher Townsville regional figure in June can be explained in part by poor jobs performances in Charter Towers (12.8 per cent), Ingham (11.9 per cent) and Palm Island (49.8 per cent).

So for all our challenges there is positive news. Townsville City is more than likely below the regional headline three-month rate of 8.8 per cent and some suburbs are well below that figure. These robust suburbs provide a strong foundation for the resilient nature of Townsville's economy and its diversified skills base.

The better job performing suburbs in Townsville represent about 50 per cent of the community and in June had a combined unemployment rate of just 3.6 per cent.

Many of these suburbs are recent additions such as Annandale, Bohle Plains, Deeragun, Kirwan West and Douglas.

They are linked to the leading employment zone in the city – the army, hospital, JCU, Myer zone.

Households in these suburbs have higher than state-average incomes, are better qualified and are more likely to work in resilient industries.

These crucial and resilient suburbs represent a large and strong component of Townsville's greater family.

I hope you get your fair share of your family on Thursday and enjoy their strengths, vulnerabilities and discuss the good old days and future fun times together.

In this OFS essay I describe the locations around Townsville that "comparatively" struggle to gain reliable consistent employment. I name them the Battler suburbs.

Battlers need a government hand

Words: 306

Townsville suburbs can be classified into three main groups: battlerburbs, vulnerburbs and resilientburbs.

As at June 2014, seven out of 25 Townsville suburbs were classified by DSEconomics as in jobs crisis and a further seven were in urgent need of attention. The remaining eleven suburbs were performing well but as the data is three months out of date, several of these suburbs could be reclassified.

Battler suburbs are generally located either close to the city or on the city outskirts. When we combined these battler zones and calculated their joint unemployment, it was more than 10 per cent (June 2014) and classified as 'in crisis'.

They include Garbutt-West End (12.3 per cent), Heatley (10.6 per cent), Gulliver-Currajong-Vincent (10.4 per cent), Condon-Rassmusen (10 per cent), Kelso (9.3 per cent), Aitkenvale (9 per cent) and Kirwan East (9 per cent).

According to government data these suburbs specialise in lower-skilled retail, wholesale, construction and transport/postal industries workers. They have lower-than-average household incomes and more part-time and casual workers, experience above-average property crime and have lower specialisation in resilient occupations.

However, much has happened since June this year and given the short-term economic horizon, the

economic and unemployment story for the largest city in North Australia is likely to remain sluggish.
I am optimistic about Townsville's economic future but unless we receive hard and fast payback for our previous contribution and future potential (or something else changes), Townsville's economic recovery will be long and painfully drawn out, possibly not even turning around until 2017.
While my economic crystal ball might be slightly foggy, one thing is certain, Townsville battlers' destinies are firmly linked to the actions of the federal and state governments, which need to act swiftly and decisively so we bolster confidence, support viable businesses and create a more diversified economy with sustainable jobs.

In this OFS essay I combine economic information about the sale of the port with political challenges; challenges that are evident in history. I point out that a state government is less likely to invest in a region that doesn't support their side of politics. I identify and describe Frame and Wedge regional politics.
"Sell a state asset that was built by a private company and if you don't support our side we wont give you the proceeds".... ***There are many other examples of this regional public investment political wedging such as the PET scanner, Blakeys crossing and Jezzine Barracks funding.*** **Its unpleasant and negative politics and poor, amateurish economic development policy.**

Bypass Brisbane for our own good

Words: 435

WE need to keep past, present and future Brisbane honest about our fair share of any proceeds from possible lease of public assets. As I analyse the language being used, if the Townsville community rejects the sale of the port by voting out some or all of the LNP representatives but the LNP resumes power (or Labor wins) in Brisbane at the next state election then there is a solid chance we could lose the lot.

There is already a strong wedge being developed by Brisbane on the lease proceeds. Conservative Brisbane could use a state wide re-election win as a mandate to sell our port but with the possibility after the next state election of three non-LNP members, they could give nothing to Townsville. Yes prepare for a protracted almighty wedge.

Why would conservative Brisbane give a massive economic boost to our region and make non-LNP members look good – politically stupid. And why would conservative Cant-berra provide funds to make non-LNP members and councillors look good? They would frame the fiscal argument such that it would be non-LNP members' and councillors' fault and wedge the community for change. Unfortunately this means long delays to boost our economy.

This scenario has a precedent. A similar situation occurred back in the 1980s when Premier Joh promised Townsville over $200 million to build a resort on Florence Bay. The community rejected the proposal and voted out Tourism Minister Max Hooper as member for Townsville. Joh was voted back in Brisbane. A bit miffed about losing Tourism Minister Max, he promptly diverted funds to other centres and also the location of the North Queensland international airport.

There are many other examples of this regional public investment political wedging such as the PET scanner, Blakeys crossing and Jezzine Barracks funding. Some of these examples took years for the different politics at different levels of government to align before the project could advance for the benefit of the people. The sooner we find a way to bypass Brisbane the better off voters in our region and the rest of North Queensland are going to be.

We need to keep past, present and future Brisbane honest about our fair share of any proceeds from possible lease of these assets. The more I hear present Brisbane say the money is going into a regional development fund with different pots of money the more I think our money could end up developing other regions, maybe even the Gold Coast. The Gold Coast or Cairns could laugh all the way to prosperity funded by Townsville with the decision made 1500km away in Brisbane.

I sometimes chose interesting language to convey the message that Our Fair Share has been created to keep the bastards honest....

Does past and present Brisbane think we are a mob of economic coprophagists, sycophantly thanking our southern political masters for the fiscal crumbs that fall from their lofty towers? I hope they had a dictionary!!

Port lease will only return us crumbs
Words: 500

WHOEVER determined 25 per cent was our fair share for the proceeds of the lease of the port, and nothing else, is economically shallow and parochially ignorant.

The Northern and North West regions could be contributing more than 10 per cent of assets for lease and receiving less than 1 per cent; hardly our fair share! Who is looking after our interests when these conversations are had in Brisbane? Does past and present Brisbane think we are a mob of economic coprophagists, sycophantly thanking our southern political masters for the fiscal crumbs that fall from their lofty towers? Is it true that the more things change in Brisbane the more they stay the same for Townsville and the North?

A long time ago I defined and created a set formula for Our Fair Share to keep local and Brisbane Labor honest. Our Fair Share is a function of population size, population growth and economic contribution: it makes sense, it's about people, how fast their community grows and how hard they work. As argued in a previous column, we need to combine the Northern and North West (NNW) regions to calculate our fair contribution so we can calculate our fair share.

Basically if we consider our population share and then allow for population growth and economic contribution, we should be entitled to around 7 per cent of the $37 billion, or about $2.5 billion. But we need to contribute our fair share to Brisbane Labor's state debt; arguably this should only be about 7 per cent; after all, the current state debt built Brisbane Labor's delirious ambition to be compared to Sydney, Melbourne or London and not Townsville facilities. Apparently, debt repayment has been predetermined at 75 per cent.

Anyway, this leaves 25 per cent, or $9.25 billion, to be distributed. Our Fair Share of this amount is about $650m. Given Brisbane's 25 per cent parameters, we won't get the $1 billion our region's mayors are asking for. After all, it could be argued that the amount we are asking for, only $1 billion, is extremely generous towards Brisbane, especially if NNW regions get less than 3 per cent and contribute more than 10 per cent. But it actually looks like we could be getting 1 per cent of any possible proceeds. We need to keep past and present Brisbane honest about our fair share of any proceeds from possible lease of public assets. Past and present Brisbane doesn't get this, but I'm sure by now all our state candidates do. We need to prosecute our fair share case harder, let Brisbane know we won't roll over and demand what's rightfully, reasonably and justifiably our fair share. Otherwise I respectfully suggest Brisbane bugger off and sell their own southern stuff to pay for their own debt. Finally, what happens if Queensland gets more than $37 billion? Do we get more or does Brisbane pocket this? What happens if we change our present representatives and the current government is returned in Brisbane?

Our Fair Share is a positive economic and powerful political tool that any region can use to prosecute for better, more reasonable, fiscal allocations.

As part of my evidence based research values, I would contact ministers and members to verify data and policy. I received many responses but usually it was general in nature, it was like I'd stumbled over information the government didn't want to discuss. Cutting APS jobs in Townsville in 2013 was similar to cutting APS jobs in 1996 – cutting economic security and diversity of Townsville, similarly, at a time when the city was economically trending down. I finish this essay with an alternative to living in the regions, we can all go live in the big cities and congest them further.

This column received many positive responses and may have saved some APS jobs in Townsville. It was still on message that the city was in recession and it was a bad time to cut important higher income jobs, where the flow

on impacts are felt across property markets, retail and tourism.

Feds doing a job on our APS numbers
Words: 478

I'D like to thank the Minister for Employment, Eric Abetz, and Mr Ewen Jones MP, for responding to my questions from last week's column.
Unfortunately their responses were of such a general nature, they were useless. Curiously, someone else provided me with more specific data on Townsville APS job numbers. It seems that in February this year we had 2035 'direct' APS workers in Townsville and 88 per cent of those jobs existed in just four departments – Human Services, Defence, Tax and GBRMPA. We have already seen 14 per cent of local jobs cut in GBRMPA recently, far higher than the national average rate.
If Townsville loses a consistent 14 per cent of its APS workforce from this round of cuts, that represents about 285, above average income, full time jobs. Direct income lost from those cuts is around $20-$30 million from the Townsville economy and substantially more in indirect incomes. This is significant given that our fair share is about 30-50 jobs and less than $2-$4 million in direct incomes.
To be fair, the Liberal Party told us they would cut 12,000 APS positions nationally before the last

election. But Mr Abietz recently revealed that by 2017 they would have cut 16,500 APS jobs, 37.5 per cent more than promised. The opposition was also going to cut the APS by 14,000 jobs.

We have to scrutinise the government's response to last week's questions and the promises it made before the election. Clearly this investigation highlights a large gap in our expectations and the need for greater regional data transparency from Cant-berra.

Townsville can only assume there are big changes ahead for our APS workforce, the indirect jobs and businesses they support, Townsville economy and property, which could slip further into slowdown, similar to our 1997-2003 event. When Howard took office around 1996 he set about cutting public servant jobs in regional locations. So much so, this action contributed (in large part) to the only net migration population loss Townsville has experienced in the past 20 years. This action contributed to a prolonged period of stagnant economic activity, recessed property markets, real wages slowed and unemployment hit 14.1 per cent.

The first column I wrote back on January 28 saw this current local APS job cutting event on the economic horizon.

Townsville doesn't want to be a mendicant entity like Tasmania, Canberra or South Australia, but we deserve our fair share of public allocations and regional data transparency. The Townsville region needs a significant fiscal injection to boost confidence, drive the economy and build the largest, most diversified city north of the Sunshine Coast.

Otherwise we may as well consider moving to overpopulated Sydney, so we too can say we have cheaper electricity, affordable insurance, better job security, better health and education services and better public facilities – oh and an unfair bias in the NRL finals.

This next column is a swipe at the federal representatives, it was a follow up to the APS jobs loss stories and it showed my bipartisan, economic improvement approach and theme - that I was willing to do what's best for my city and region..... ***Cant-berra has a problem with the message its sending North Queenslanders. When you work hard and contribute we are one, but when your economic resilience is tested, look to others for salvation.*** **Our representative seemed like Cantberras voice in Townsville rather than Townsville's' Voice in Cantberra.**

This series of columns has the first appearance of Cant-berra. In this column we also see that the federal government is not responding to my request for information. When the story doesn't suit them don't respond.

North deserves more from its pollies

Words: 412

DON'T let the economic headlights knock you down like a startled cane toad; times are tough in Australia's largest northern city and they are going to get tougher, at least in the short term.

When I polish up my Australian-made economic crystal ball and look at the Townsville jobs market, the challenges outweigh the opportunities. The highest unemployment rate in Queensland, with a three-month average of 10 per cent, youth unemployment over 20 per cent, indigenous unemployment over 15 per cent, over-50s unemployment climbing and under-employment endemic.

Over the coming months, the events season will stall, school leavers will start looking for work, the wet season will slow what local construction activity there is, hinder mining and transport and reduce tourism and associated activity. Then there's the state election effect that will dampen both business and consumer confidence.

Recently, coal mines in the Galilee Basin shed around 1000 jobs due mainly to a world glut of coal, and last Wednesday the Australian Public Service revealed an annualised cut of 8000 jobs; around half were from natural attrition.

So I asked our four local federal representatives about the gross and net APS job change in Townsville over the past 12 months. Mr Christensen and Mr Katter's offices responded they would follow up.

Nationally, the Government expects the public service will reduce by 16,500 staff before July 2017. It means another 8575 public service jobs will go nationally over the next three years.
I also asked two supplementary questions.
Can you tell me how many of these future APS job losses are earmarked for Townsville?
Can you let me know what you are doing to stimulate the Townsville economy and create sustainable jobs in Townsville in the next 12 months?
As thousands of new job seekers enter the market and become eligible to vote, we hear that our economic compass should point more to China than Cant-berra. While I agree China should be on our economic radar, pointing our compass to China is simplistic and fraught with many challenges.
Cant-berra has a problem with the message its sending North Queenslanders. When you work hard and contribute we are one, but when your economic resilience is tested, look to others for salvation.
Cant-berra needs to quantify the contribution North Queensland makes to the Federal Budget and then recognise our fair share of fiscal allocations. It also needs to provide a cost-of-living index for Townsville, and a regional Australian representative on the monetary policy-important RBA board.

This next OFS essay is an economic story that provides important information about individual incomes in Townsville. I started providing

individual income information to the media from the mid 2000's. It's another piece in the big picture, economic puzzle that reveals Townsville's strengths, weaknesses, risks and opportunities.

ATO figures paint a pretty picture

Words: 348

THE latest Australian Taxation Office mean individual incomes figures reveal Townsville's richest location, the diversification in the location of our incomes, our public purse contribution and that we are a generous community.

We are a proud city, a confident region and a cohesive community that delivers, rarely complains and serves its country beyond expectations.

In 2012 about 90,000 Townsville workers generated almost $6 billion in gross incomes. The city's mean individual income in 2011-12 was higher than the state and national average income.

Postcode 4810 is Townsville's highest income locality with mean incomes in the top 16 per cent of Australia's postcodes.

Postcode 4814 has the largest number of workers in Townsville and our highest gross income. This postcode is the city's leading employment zone with retail, health, security and innovative precincts.

Postcode 4819 had the lowest mean individual incomes in Townsville.

But it also had the best chance to capitalise on the wave of baby boomers considering retirement dwellings and affordable lifestyle.
Our more affordable suburbs of Kirwan and Bohle Plains have the second largest number of workers in the city.
They contribute almost $1 billion in gross incomes.
In the seven years from 2005 to 2012 the number of taxable individuals living in Townsville grew by 17 per cent, our mean individual incomes grew by 43.2 per cent and our median house price also grew by 42 per cent.
As a city we paid $74 million to the Medicare levy and 53 per cent of workers have private health insurance. Townsville workers paid almost $1.2 billion in PAYE tax to the Federal Government.
For a long time Townsville has contributed its fair share to the public purse and there is evidence that we are a generous community who donate above the state average.
We are a community that rarely complains but when we do there's usually evidence to support it.
But there is a self-fulfilling Townsville saying that we are the most diversified and resilient regional economy in regional Australia. And as most long term Townsvillians know, our determination, innovation and perspiration will facilitate a rebound.

Using metaphors is a good way of conveying a message. Politicians use them all the time, economists are less inclined to use them, probably because they are emotionally based

and we aren't trained to manipulate emotions, just provide information.

I use a metaphor in this column to convey the message that the north contributes significantly but doesn't get fiscally recognized in return; it's a combination of economic information and emotional persuasion.... ***But I think there's a deeper challenge, we're letting the neighbors pick the low-hanging fruit from our orchards, not charging full price at the gate and not planting additional tropical fruit trees to diversify the northern orchard!***

South bleeding the North dry

Words: 231

NORTH Queenslanders are not the only Australians disgruntled with the sharing of wealth created from the northern mining boom.

We can sympathise with Western Australians, who are angry the state's hard-earned dollars are going to other states.

Western Australia loses $3.7 billion a year, of which $500 million to Tasmania, $750 million goes to South Australia, but incredibly $600 million to Queensland (I wonder how much makes it past the Tropic of Capricorn?) and $140 million to Canberra.

In 2013, Western Australians contributed $102,232 per person to the national economy, Canberrans $90,631, North Queenslanders $84,705 (2011),

Northern Territorians $83,828. The average Australian contribution was $66,549.
If we exclude the unproductive Capital Territory, then the three top contributors per person are arguably all in North Australia.
North Queensland is arguably the second-highest contributor to the national economy.
I say this because just about every Canberran business is a parasite on the public sector and on the taxpayers of Australia.
I agree with Western Australians.
But I think there's a deeper challenge, we're letting the neighbours pick the low-hanging fruit from our orchards, not charging full price at the gate and not planting additional tropical fruit trees to diversify the northern orchard!
I also believe the system needs a good service because the landlords are charging too much rent and not fully maintaining the farm, let alone developing and innovating the northern orchard.

In 2013 I point out that all the members of the RBA Board, Australia's monetary policy making body, live in capital cities. None of the past Board members lived in regional locations. With 30% of Australias population and the producer of most of our exports, I suggest someone from regional Australia should be appointed to the RBA Board....*After*

contributing our fair share over the past half century, it's time a regional Australian resident was appointed to the Reserve Bank Board. Only this way can a third of Australia's population be confident that monetary policy decisions are including them.

Let us have our say on fiscal future
Words: 357

IT'S interest rate day today, and it's time to prosecute a case for a regional Australian to become a member of the Reserve Bank Board. Not one of the nine members of the Reserve Bank board lives in regional Australia. Not one of the past members of the monetary policy making body has ever lived in regional Australia. How can the RBA board make a decision on behalf of all Australians if they haven't experienced the conditions in some of those locations?

Regional Australia comprises a third of Australia's population, contributes most of its exports and many of its tourism destinations. In the past decade regional Australia with its mining industry kept recession and depression from Australia's door.

Next year will be the first chance for a regional Australian to join the RBA board and express regional Australia's rational expectation regarding monetary policy and interest rates. In December 2015 Roger Corbett's position comes up for re-election. Following that Catherine Tanna's position

is available on March 29, 2016, followed by John Akhurst's role on July 30, 2016. Two other positions become available in 2017.
In total there are nine members of the RBA board with six non-executive members appointed by the Treasurer. The non-executive members are appointed for terms of up to five years. There is no limit on the number of terms a member may serve.
Are all the previous federal governments saying that there is no regional Australian who has the calibre to be appointed to the board? Next year, surely presents an opportunity for the current federal government to change this value judgement, and ensure regional Australia has a say in monetary policy decisions.
There are many worthy regional Australian contenders for this challenging role and some of them live in Townsville including Company director Russell Laird, James Cook University Deputy Vice Chancellor Chris Cocklin and Chamber of Commerce president Stephen Moti.
After contributing our fair share over the past half century, it's time a Townsville and regional Australian resident was appointed to the Reserve Bank Board. Only this way can a third of Australia's population be confident that monetary policy decisions are including them.

Townsville is a region that has more than the average state percentage of indigenous residents. They find it harder to obtain and keep work. Palm Island has around 50%

unemployment rate, yet it has so much opportunity. Many indigenous families live with poor health, poor education and in poverty. Our Fair Share includes everyone and the concepts can be applied to all communities to obtain better outcomes.

On a visit to Palm Island in 2016 I heard the local mayors plan to capture trade from passing sailing boats. There is now a retail centre that will help with this plan.

Palm Islands key to employment
Words: 321

ABORIGINAL and Torres Strait Islander residents contribute to the prosperity and diversity of Townsville regions economy, environment and resilient community. However ATSI unemployment remains higher than the general regional population and more education take up and specific industry development is required.
But there is a special place that could open entrepreneurial doors creating hundreds of jobs and boosting the diversity of our economy. The Palm Islands are an exotic playground waiting to be developed and alive with curiosity. Could the Palms be the next big tourism opportunity for an adventure hungry world to enjoy?
According to the 2011 census Townsville region specialises in Aboriginal and Torres Strait Islander

residents. In 2011 there were 15,412 ATSI resident in wider Townsville. This represents almost 10 per cent of the state ATSI population and 1.5 per cent of the national ATSI population. Overall, the Townsville region represents 5.1 per cent of the Queensland population and 0.8 per cent of the national population.

By 2026 the local ATSI population is estimated by DS Economics to increase by about 50 per cent to 23,238 residents. Education and entrepreneurial opportunities are positive pathways.

In 2011, Townsville region ATSI resident's median age was 20, almost half the age of other Townsvillians, which was 34. The life expectancy, health and education of ATSI Townsvillians need better consideration from state and federal governments.

Townsville region has our fair share of ATSI residents. Like any distinct group of residents they present opportunities and challenges. So how do we provide access to the ownership of the factors of production so ATSI people not only have a job they own businesses, investment assets and have role models that inspire future generations?

One solution involves developing the Palm Islands. North East Bay, Phantom Island and Curacao Island are uninhabited exotic adventure tourism opportunities with beautiful beaches, rainforest and fringing coral reefs. The Palms are Northern Queensland's Caribbean waiting to be enjoyed by tourists worldwide

After cyclone Yasi in 2011, I started a community clean up day. I organized a group of 16 PNG international students and helped older people in Hermit Park. They helped over 20 households on their first outing. This suburb clean up day continued each year until 2016 when I organized 40 international students helped clean up the top of Castle Hill.

I use the following essay to remind Brisdrain that regional Queensland is part of the state, is a big contributor and that regional locations have expectations regarding state public investment and jobs.

Many happy returns on Budget day?
Words: 406

FIRSTLY a follow up from last week's column, several people suggested raising the littering fine to $5000; a good suggestion that is part of the long-term solution.
Also one group of international students studying in Townsville offered to clean up our mess. What a wonderful positive gesture from people who aren't from Townsville but have pride in this city.
If you belong to a local community or sporting group we may be able to help with your clean-up. I look forward to helping clean up Townsville with this group.
To other matters – Happy State Budget Day. State budgets aren't the same as federal fiscal plans. It's

sort of deciding which one is better, Australian cricket or Sheffield Shield? Sorry for the rhetorical question.

Last month we heard Minister Trad tell Brisdrain that the major component of the state Budget this year would include three projects, all in SEQ.

They included an extension of light rail on the Gold Coast; new rail to the Sunny Coast and another bridge across the Brisdrain River.

Why Minister Trad announced these initiatives and not the Premier or Treasurer is curious.

What state public investment is the Brisdrain Government putting into the Magnetic Coast region to drive economic growth, create jobs and boost confidence?

The wider Townsville region (Northern and North West) is a unique area with a growing population, diversified economy and unique challenges.

The wider region has a broadbased economy with significant manufacturing, mining, agriculture, world-class education facilities; the largest regional hospital in Queensland; a deep water access port that is a world leader in refined base metal and sugar exports; largest army barracks in Australia and significant environmental assets.

The Northern and North West region is the most diversified economy in North Queensland. This diversification will encourage jobs growth in the future and improve net migration. The economic contribution of the NNW is about $20 billion or around 7 per cent of the state's economy. Our

economic contribution is a significant component of Our Fair Share of state public investment.
The wider Townsville region also has many competitive and strategic advantages compared to other regional cities that complement a promising future; its access to affordable water; vast affordable and appropriate industrial and residential land; a better educated and skilled workforce; a deep water access port but baseload power prices for industry are a challenge.
All we basically ask for is Our Fair Share from tonight's state Budget.

In the following OFS essay I attack a higher cost of living statement in the Northern Development white paper. I have a strong background on regional grocery price index, petrol price advocacy and property research.

The North Australia white paper is a positive step forward. It's the first plan of its kind. But if it is to be successful, its data needs to support the conclusion. This being true, the only conclusion I can draw from the cost of living motherhood statement is that cantberra doesn't know our cost of living, doesn't know our cost to do business and needs to revisit this statement to connect with most people in the North, and talk up potential economic-driving deals that benefit all Australians.

Cost of living figure bit of guesswork

Words: 491

HAPPY end of financial year and here's to a more sustainably prosperous next financial year with more opportunities, more jobs and lower costs. Here's to a more confident Magnetic Coast.

There was an interesting article in last Friday's *Bulletin* about households north of Bowen (another definition of North Queensland) being the best savers in Queensland.

One conclusion was that a higher cost of living was the key reason why people save better in the North. Another might be households saving for a rainy day.

Anyway, this high cost of living notion seems to be reinforced by the recent North Australia white paper which states that the North has much higher living costs than the south and was a deterrent for people and business to move here.

I'm amazed they can make such a shallow statement when the only official inflation figure in North Australia is captured on the fourth largest city in the North – Little Darwin.

Other evidence disputes this comparatively higher cost of living notion in the North East. The most recent State Government cost of living report showed that places such as Townsville, Charter

Towers, Burdekin and Ingham are among the cheapest locations in Queensland.

The Federal Government can't make motherhood statements that effect commercial decisions and population movements without valid evidence-based foundation.

Truth is it doesn't know our costs and it's probably been listening to draw conclusion, rather than collecting and analysing.

To be sure, Darwin, the Northern Territory and the North West are higher-cost locations but the North East, where most of the North's population and economic diversity exists, is not in the same classification.

There's evidence that suggests we might be comparatively cheaper than the south, but we won't know until we do the economic analysis.

Every budget is different but in general accommodation costs are most Australians highest expense.

Townsville regions' median home prices are about 70 per cent cheaper than Sydney's and over a third cheaper than the national median home price.

As a consequence, our average mortgages are lower. Our average rents are much lower than the capital city average, including Darwin.

There are many other examples of lower costs. There are many examples of higher costs such as petrol, home insurance and marginal costs of base load power for high-end business users.

The North Australia white paper is a positive step forward. It's the first plan of its kind. But if it is to be

successful, its data needs to support the conclusion. This being true, the only conclusion I can draw from the cost of living motherhood statement is that Cantberra doesn't know our cost of living, doesn't know our cost to do business and needs to revisit this statement to connect with most people in the North, and talk up potential economic-driving deals that benefit all Australians.
Bottom line is include North Queensland in the quarterly or annual CPI figures and we will all be in a better position.

This next OFS essay is a tongue in cheek column that makes light of the budget as the economic Grand Final and the federal treasurers comment about the north being the great frontier!! I present key economic evidence to draw a conclusion about North Australia Investment Fund -NAIF.

In 2014 I was contacted by a development organization with the results of a long awaited feasibility study, completed by the LNP – I remember my steadfast discussion with the shadow Treasurer in 2008/09, now treasurer about this need for competitively priced baseload power in North Queensland!!

It's time to stop milking our cash cow
Words: 480

I HAD several people contact me last week and ask if they could join me for the Economic Grand Final.
Rather than say no, I suggested we look to the future and consider next year's fiscal grand final party and meet at a local pub, like The Herbert. I predict the same sides will compete next year.
It's great for the North to be recognised twice in the past five years in the Economic Grand Final.
For too long the North was a forgotten cash cow, but we are slowly changing that attitude. Joe Hockey now recognises North Australia as the Great Frontier.
North Australia is a land where families work hard and smart, just like anywhere else in Australia, but each man, woman and child contributes more than double what southern Aussies do to the national economy. On average, each North Australian contributes $140,000 to our economy, while the average person on the southern side of the Tropic of Capricorn contributes just $59,000.
North Australia as a region contributes double that of South Australia to the economy, with a similar population, and seven times that of Tasmania, with just less than triple the population. Within 20 years it is likely that the North will have a greater population than these two states combined. Yet they have 24 senators and 17 MPs between them, and we have eight "full" MP electorates and five senators.
With 5.5 per cent of Australia's population, North Australia contributes almost 12 per cent of Australia's economy. This would also mean we

contribute more per person in government revenue than the southern part of Australia. If we contribute so much and we are part of Australia's Great Frontier, why should we have such low federal representation?

In North Australia, North Queensland has the largest share of population; Townsville is the largest city in the North and will remain so for the foreseeable future. It's curious that a Northern Alliance group (Cairns, Darwin and Broome) has been created, apparently without much consultation with the largest city in the North? Maybe we need to start a different Northern partnership – one that unites all North Australia and includes Townsville, Mackay, Rockhampton, Alice Springs and the Pilbara Development Commission? We might even be inclusive and invite the other three cities.

So with North Australia's $178 billion economic contribution, is the $5 billion concessional loan fund part of our long-run fair share? It's a piece in the economic development puzzle, but in a world of low-interest loans it's more about feasible projects than the cost of them. The fund is essentially a Christmas hamper without any food in it.

Recently, a feasibility study was released that concluded a baseload power station in North Queensland was viable. But we need the Queensland Government to recognise this project as a priority for northern economic development and be part of this Great Frontier.

In this essay from 2014 I raise the Olympics bid issue by South East Queensland. I remember the public investment challenges in regional Queensland from the commonwealth games and allow the reader to draw their own conclusion about supporting another larger sporting event.
"Great for the South East but potentially disastrous for regional Queensland. ***I fail to see how any significant positive development will occur north of the Fitzroy River from this bid led by a maverick group of southern councils."***

Northern exposure to Olympics bid
Words: 407

THE next Olympic Games will be held in Rio de Janeiro in Brazil next year, with the 2020 Games to take place in Tokyo, Japan. Now we hear that a coalition or union of southeast Queensland governments is seeking the 2028 Olympic Games.
Centred on "Brisdrain", the potential host region will span from the Gold Coast to Toowoomba up to the Sunshine Coast.
This sounds like a great plan for the southeast, but what does it mean for North Queensland?
The potential marketing spin will promote southeast Queensland surrounding Brisdrain.

For the first time in history, a small regional pitch to host the Olympics will be made as opposed to a single city-based bid.

One concern I have is that public investment will be concentrated and sustained for a decade or more in the southeast corner to the detriment of the rest of Queensland.

Remember, on a per person basis North Queenslanders from Rockhampton north contribute far more to GDP than southeast Queensland residents.

Sunshine Coast Mayor Mark Jamieson said: "I think it's absolute collaboration and co-operation between the (SEQ) council of mayors that will be our secret weapon in doing something like that essentially for the first time."

The 2028 Olympics is only 13 years away, the time to be planning for that opportunity would need to start now. What does this mean for the state's budget and other regional Queensland locations?

The Sunshine Coast Mayor went on to say, "It's part of the plan to see significant infrastructure development in Queensland".

I fail to see how any significant positive development will occur north of the Fitzroy River from this bid led by a maverick group of southern councils.

But I can see that we northerners will be disrupted by lower public investment, slower project delivery, higher state public debt (that we all have to pay for) and the potential changes to daylight savings.

Basically, if you want to concentrate on the Olympics, Queensland can't have balanced fiscal distributions. If this SEQ-centric plan goes ahead, state public investment will more than ever be focused on the southeast corner and federal public investment will more than likely compliment it.
We either get on board and let the southeast benefit, prosecute a case against it or bargain for inclusion – being a friend with benefits.
Bottom line: The southeast can't have its Olympic cake and eat it if it wants to be part of the whole Queensland community.

In the following essay I ridicule the Lord Mayor of Brisbane about his comments dividing SEQ and Regional Queensland.... *fellow mangoes, we should be grateful to Brisdrain for our lower education standards, lower regional life expectancy, higher unemployment levels and the higher marginal cost of petrol and electricity. Enjoy*

Brisdrain short-changing the North
Words: 412

SOMEONE asked me recently why I call Brisbane, Brisdrain. I have many friends in the far southeast and some of my family live there, crikey I've lived there; it's a bonza place. I love my family and I like the people of Brisdrain; we are all Australians. But the southern decision-making class are a fiscal drain on each northern person's economic contribution.

Like it or not, southern decision makers have the ear of State Treasury and most ministers. In a 2015 Queensland State Election promotion document, Council of Mayors South East Queensland chairman Cr Graham Quirk said the southeast was Queensland's economic driver and deserved the biggest slice of funding.

I am skeptical when such sweeping statements are made. Quantify biggest slice please Cr Quirk! They deserve a fair share of funding, but to declare the southeast as the state's economic driver is ignorant.

Remember the two-speed economy? Where is most mining activity located Cr Quirk?

To proclaim that the southeast is the only, or key driver of the Queensland economy is provincially one dimensional. If Sydney or Melbourne made a similar announcement would he agree that they deserved an unquantified biggest share of federal public funding?

Cr Quirk's statement went on to say, "At its simplest, investment in Queensland's regions cannot be at the expense of Queensland's core growth region or all will lose out. If southeast Queensland works, Queensland works". Fail, Cr Quirk, because public investment needs to be determined by population and productivity.

Then he fails bigger than Nixon's relationship with the truth, "It is not unreasonable to comment that the high standard of living across our state – and the desirability and attractiveness of our state to new businesses and residents – has come predominantly from the successful, ongoing growth of southeast Queensland." Yep, fellow mangoes, we should be grateful to Brisdrain for our lower education standards, lower regional life expectancy, higher unemployment levels and the higher marginal cost of petrol and electricity. Then while he's touring the state he can tell our miners, grazing companies and tourist facility owners that they are here because of the southeast.

These statements diminish the value of North Queensland and divide Queensland. There are almost a million people living north of Rockhampton who contribute around $80 billion in economic activity. Economically we don't need the southeast but they need us.

North Queensland is a far more productive region than the southeast acknowledges, and we deserve our fair share of public funding.

I seek the truth through economics and I persuade through evidence based research. In one of my final columns I recongnise the changes in economics over the past 150 years and acknowledge that GDP has faults. I revisit my student days and how time changes lives. I also discuss a philosopher hero of mine, Diogenes.

There is more to life than money

Words: 305

THERE are people out there wealthier than you and I but guess what, there could be happier people out there too!

There is a proverb that I like, “the first generation develops the wealth the second consolidates it and the third squanders it”. I question; “but which generation had the most fun?”

Back in the 1800s economists used to calculate a population’s happiness rather than their productivity.

Gross domestic product is a 20th century invention. Economics has changed a lot in 200 years.

Today there are countries such as Bhutan that use a Gross National Happiness Index to gauge how their people are progressing.

They define it as the peace and happiness of people and security and sovereignty of the nation.

No measure of productivity is going to measure how happy our community is or give governments indicators to implement policies that support community wellbeing.

The current measure believes if you’ve got a job, you’re occupied; less likely to revolt and simultaneously you’re happily contributing to the progress of the nation.

I’d like to share one of the happiest times in my life. It was when I was a poor university student living in a share house. I owned a bike, desk, mattress and some clothes. I struggled to pay for food, sport, rent and electricity, but always seemed to manage. I also had a student loan that probably saw my net wealth as below zero.

Over time and with a growing family my needs changed.
I'm not about to adopt a Diogenes existence again but as a community we need to measure how we are progressing with our health, our schooling and community vitality as much as our jobs, inflation and exports. Life is not about how much money or possessions you have. Life is about fun and getting our fair share of it.

The following essay highlights the ever common use of the term Our Fair Share and how it can be spun into an alternative frame and wedge very quickly.

Some people suggest that my contribution to regional economics has been significant and diverse. That my contribution to regional politics and the art of persuasion has been enormous with close to 900 individual appearances in the Townsville Bulletin and thousands of appearances in other mainstream media platforms over 20 years.

Very few people would have had this much influence over such a long time.

More to Queensland than southeast
Words: 467

I DON'T normally read the *Courier Mail* because it's a southern paper and its main purpose is supplying information to the southeast corner. Then on July 21 the front page photo with an Australian surfer being harassed by a South African great white shark caught my attention.

As if the Springboks didn't organise that shark to be at Jeffreys Bay the day after we controversially beat them in the Gabba rugby Test!

Two close calls, but it was on page 22 that it went downhill from an inspirational story to a hypocritical letter to the editor from our Premier.

She criticised the federal government for apparently denying Queensland $1 billion for infrastructure projects. The money was tied to privatisation of assets and because we as a state rejected that policy the Federal Government is denying us a fair share. The feds can't just change its rules and make one rule for us and another rule for everyone else. Methinks she's playing sharks in a smaller pool.

Unsurprisingly, she accuses the Federal Government of stubbornness. This could be seen as hypocritical and a pointless prosecution pathway but it makes her appear like she's standing up to Cantberra.

To her credit she compares Queensland to Western Australia's concessional funding due to reduced mining royalties, and rightfully points out that Queensland has had a $3 billion reduction in mining royalties with no similar compensation program from the Federal Government.

Good argument and good economics! But is she fighting for all Queensland or just the southeast?
Our Premier says Queenslanders deserve a fair share of their own tax dollars. Great to see that she and her party are keen to be part of sharing the public investment and recurrent expenditure pie equally.
Does she believe in payback for short-changing the North in the past? Our Premier can't have it both ways. Arguing for a fair share from the feds but not distributing it fairly to Queensland regions is hypocritical politics and poor economics.
Equal fiscal distribution is a long-term equation.
Our local federal member has consistently said the Federal Government rarely and sparingly funds stadiums and recently pointed out that Brisdrain governments had almost fully funded several southeast Queensland stadiums for football, netball and $1.5 billion for Gold Coast stadiums. It's the challenge we have due to our distance from the seat of power. Brisdrain is willing to contribute less than half ($100 million) to Townsville's proposed stadium. He asked whether anyone has asked local representatives why Brisdrain won't fund most of our stadium as they do down south.

It appears Brisdrain Labor believes in one set of rules for the southeast and another for the Fitzroy River North. Here's your chance to reply, local MPs. Shouldn't Townsville and the northwest get a similar deal as the southeast for stadium funding?

Conclusion to Part 2

This collection of Our Fair Share essays, published in Townsville Bulletin from 2013 to 2015 were designed to inform and inspire regional Queenslanders to think differently about their total contribution, how it should be invested and who should make those public investment decisions. These articles were also written to inform and influence decision makers about Townsville, North Queensland and regional Queensland.

The collection was divided into Political, Population and Society, Tourism and Economics essays. Combined, I felt they created a powerful influential resource for regional people of North Queensland and Townsville, then, now and into the future.

I accomplished more than I expected, informing and educating thousands of people about public investment decisions, influencing regional politics and prosecuting public finance fairness. The influence the term has, is across states and through nations.

Our Fair Share is an 'ecoonomic-political' tool that can change quality of regional people's lives for the better.

5 PART 3 INFLUENCE OF OUR FAIR SHARE

The author was the first economist to use the term 'Our Fair Share' and define it in its current form. I was also the first political candidate to use the slogan 'Our Fair Share'. I used it strategically in Townsville Bulletin, following up this publicity in a candidate endorsement speech in 2008 and the Our Fair Share Logo in a Queensland state election in 2009. From my research this was the first time the term Our Fair Share was used by a candidate in a political campaign.

The economic term for Our Fair Share is Regional Horizontal Fiscal Equalisation (RHFE). RHFE is a derivative of commonwealth state fiscal relations in Australia. RHFE, first defined by me, was founded on public infrastructure investment but grew to include economic contributions and their forecasts, population size and changes, and importantly political representation equity.

I feel I have had, and the evidence confirms, significant influence over significant decision makers in Australia for a long time and that the term will last into the future. Many others have used the term for their advantage in economics, politics and social and community organisations.

I defined Our Fair Share in economic and demographic terms and applied it to Queensland state budget analysis between 2006 and 2019, with the help of journalist Tony Raggatt. During this time different State governments indicated regions where getting Our Fair Share from the State Budget. I remain skeptical and more research is required to confirm or deny their claim.

The slogan, Our Fair Share is now in common use. Economists are using the term and more journalists have been and are asking questions using the term. The collaboration of journalist, economist and politician are crucial to the success and vast influence of the term Our Fair Share.

From 2013 to 2015 I wrote a Column in the Townsville Bulletin titled Our Fair Share. This weekly column was focused on economics and politics with some light social stories that mixed the column up. In general, the theme of the column followed on from my initial campaign of Townsville not receiving a fair share of Public Investment given population (Per capita), Population growth, Economic contribution and Economic growth.

I will continue to use the Twitter handle of Our Fair Share and linkedin profile indicates that I am the founder of 'Our Fair Share" method and of the concept regional horizontal fiscal equalisation.

INFLUENCE and SUCCESS

The influence of the Our Fair Share term has been wide and enduring. It has initiated discussion and debate amongst economists and is widely used in the media. It has been used by politicians and decision makers and it has positively influenced regional public investment decisions.

Politicians that have used the term Our Fair Share widely, include George Christiansen (NAT), Dale Last (LIB), Senator Ian Macdonald (Lib), Terri Butler (ALP), Cathy OToole maiden speech to parliament (ALP), Bob Katter (KAP), Robbie Katter (KAP), Shane Kunth (KAP), Independent Cairns 2016 Slogan, Peter Lindsay (LIB), Evette Darth (ALP 2019), Victorian Premier Andrews (ALP 2019), many State and local government candidates.

Media that have used the term or a derivative of it with the same meaning NEWS Corp regional papers and AIP.

I stood for the seat of Herbert at the 2016 Federal election, prior to this Federal election the sitting member had a safe seat with a margin of 6 points. The major parties weren't interested in spending in a safe seat!!! As a candidate in an election that was determined by preferences, I know I had an influence on several projects, which created thousands of local jobs.

Townsville Bulletin played a strong role in the Townsville **Our Fair Share** Campaign. Other media played their part also, including ABC Radio, Seven Local News, WIN local News and national papers and national TV news.

I hope other regions around Australia can benefit from this unique strategic economic-political approach and gain appropriate fiscal recognition.

6 CONCLUSION

Dwyers Our Fair Share slogan and campaign has had significant influence in media and with decision makers. Its success is due to the simplicity of the slogan and the different ways (political, economic, demographic) it can be used.

I developed it in 2005/06 possibly earlier and in reference to State public investment shares in regional Queensland. I collaborated with respected journalist, Tony Raggatt, in the Townsville Bulletin to convey the slogan and economic message. Together we made a significant difference over a decade and a half, and possibly beyond.

The term is now used by Prime Ministers, State premiers, local government councillors but most importantly it is understood by everyday people as a tool to describe regional horizontal fiscal equalisation. As my thesis supervisor once said "simplify it and they will understand."

My Our Fair Share column finished in 2015. The real value of the information was to provide quality well sourced information for the people of North Queensland and Townsville, who were being underfunded, undervalued and politically, economically, and socially disrespected. Which comes to the next instalment in Our Fair Share, should there be a New State?

In 2019 I gave a presentation to the Economic Society of Australia in Townsville. The topic was a New State Test in Australia and it was based on the Royal Commission into the New State referendum in Northern New South Wales in 1967.

Dwyers New state test requires additional research and is a good foundation for any undervalued region in Australia, looking for 'Our Fair Share'.

7 APPENDIX 1 ECONOMIC SOCIETY OF AUSTRALIA PRESENTATION

In my Existential NQ essay above (2008), I used three key variables to determine if an area had a comparative claim to section 124 of the Constitution. Below I expand this set of variables to seven, with each variable having horizontal and vertical stratification.

As founder of Our Fair Share and Regional Economist, I was recently invited to present to the Economic Society of Australia (ESA). The purpose of the presentation was to develop and discuss a reliable, broad test for a *New State,* anywhere in Australia.

Over the years, I have collected comprehensive information about North Queensland. So, I chose New North Queensland as the test area. My boundary for New North Queensland includes the historical five statistical divisions of Far North, Northern, North West, Mackay and Fitzroy, an area I defined as North Queensland in 2008.

A summary of findings from my ESA presentation follow.

Dwyer's New State Test includes

- population,
- economic activity,
- ownership of and need for social assets,
- common interest in the community,
- distance from existing capital,
- risk assessment and a
- precautionary test.

Dwyer's New State Test found sufficient population in New NQ for a new state, with almost 1 million residents.

Unsurprisingly, there was significant common interest in New North Queensland community with distinctive climate, unique environmental assets and current state dividing home insurance challenges, to name a few.

New NQ zone sufficiently complied with the economic activity requirements of my test. In addition, a preliminary but comprehensive NEW NQ state budget (first of its kind), revealed New NQ would have a surplus. Other economic benefits included, gaining direct responsibility for federal funding, a seat at COAG (now disbanded) and relocation of some significant private sector company head offices from Brisbane to NQ regions; shifting considerable population and incomes.

A key area for further investigation was the ownership of State Debt and the transfer of the past sale of public assets from the north ($6B rail sale to Aurizon) to the south (2011 floods).

I found little evidence that a new state would require a 'significant' increase in public servants because, in most cases, they already exist. But there may be a relocation of a moderate number of public servants from Brisbane to North Queensland, to manage direct federal funding; once again shifting population and incomes.

With probable population shifts, the potential for Brisbane include a reduction in traffic congestion, reduced requirement to build expensive inefficient tunnels and economic benefits from daylight saving. However, one disadvantage was that

Southern Queensland would probably start out with a deficit budget before adapting.

The research identified political net benefits for a new state such as representatives delivering better 'dedication', rather than being seen as a Southern voice in the North. It also identified there may be 6 to 12 NQ senators (3 to 9 new senators). Any more than six senators and the other founding states would likely obtain more senators, and few people want more politicians.

A new State legislative assembly would depend on the type of state parliamentary system, so after discussing this with several academics, I found there could be a no net gain in state representatives and possibly a reduction.

This is a summary of the presentation, and of course we should ask, if there are new states in Australia, what are the risks and how could they be managed?

The message from the presentation, was to keep an open mind, and present credible, comprehensive evidence from reliable sources.

In conclusion, Dwyer's New State Test found that a NEW North Queensland satisfied political, most economic variable (more work required), social, technological, cultural and legal tests, that the federal government was providing considerable support for regional state public investment and that a democratic Queensland parliament would be justified in allowing northern people decide their own future.

ABOUT THE AUTHOR

Colin has a keen interest in Regional affairs. He stood for two parliaments at different elections, using the slogan Our Fair Share. He ran his own successful economic consulting business and has an honors degree in Economics.

He contributes to his local and international community. He is currently a member of the board for charity Flourishing Women, has been a member of Townsville Cricket board, JCUNQRUFC vice president and on the committee that brought the British Lions to Townsville. He was chair of the NQ Wetlands festival, founder of NQ Eco Banking and of course, Our Fair Share.

Colin has written two fact based books one on regional economics and the other on computing. He has written two separate columns in News Corp papers; an economics/property column and Our Fair Share.

Apart from interests in Politics, Economics and his community, Colin is a keen sportsman. He played first division soccer for Redlands as a fifteen year old, ran at state athletic trials, played first cricket for his school, grade cricket in Townsville and A grade rugby in Townsville. Has has coached various sports.

Colin is happy he helped make 'Our Fair Share' a household term. Knowledge is finite but imagination is everywhere.

Made in United States
Cleveland, OH
05 November 2026

47664963R10143